Balance of Power

James R. Lucas

AMACOM
American Management Association
New York • Atlanta • Boston • Chicago • Kansas City • San Francisco • Washington, D.C.
Brussels • Mexico City • Tokyo • Toronto

This book is available at a special
discount when ordered in bulk quantities.
For information, contact Special Sales Department,
AMACOM, a division of American Management Association,
1601 Broadway, New York, NY 10019.

Library of Congress Cataloging-in-Publication Data

Lucas, J. R. (James Raymond), 1950–
    Balance of power / James R. Lucas.
        p.   cm.
    Includes bibliographical references and index.
    ISBN 0-8144-0393-X (hbk.)
        1. Organizational effectiveness.   2. Power (Social sciences)
    3. Industrial management—Employee participation.   I. Title.
HD58.9.L85   1998
658.3'14—dc21   97-46428
                                                                  CIP

Printing number

10   9   8   7   6   5   4   3   2   1

To my mother
Anna Laverne Ryan Lucas

And to my brothers and sister
John Ernest Lucas
Daniel Kenneth Lucas
Timothy Michael Lucas
Mary Patricia Lucas Buecker

Together, we learned a lot about the balance of power.

Contents

Acknowledgments

I want to sincerely thank all the professionals who have given me such wonderful intellectual nourishment through the many months during which this book was being prepared. This starts with the writers whose books are listed in the Recommended Reading section in the back of this book. Although I haven't met all of you, I am certainly grateful for your labors of love. I am also thankful for what I have learned from and with my clients.

Once again, I want to express my appreciation to Walt Lantzy, a great friend, terrific colleague, and dedicated professional. Walt is a great source both of information and of inspiration. He reviewed the manuscript and shared some excellent insights. I don't know where you came from, Walt, but if I find out I'm going to see if they have any more like you.

Many thanks to my colleagues John Hughes and Dale Mask, who graciously took time out of their relentless schedules to review this book in draft form and provide excellent suggestions and thoughtful comments. It's a better book because of you.

My support staff, led by Janette Jasperson, made this a doable and better work. Janette did a fabulous job of substantive and detailed editing, peppering the early drafts with excellent questions, comments, and suggestions. Her ability to decipher my handwriting on review copies should qualify her for an honorary degree in hieroglypics. Maryl Janson added to the effort with some superb questions and insights.

I want to thank my daughter Laura, who edited the book in detail and keeps me hopping intellectually. My son Peter, a real computer whiz, provided technical support to me and the rest of the staff. David and Bethany, my youngest two, provided a lot of enthusiasm and exuberance. My thanks to Pam and all of my family and friends for their support and encouragement.

For two books in a row, I have had the privilege of working with Adrienne Hickey, my editor at AMACOM. She is a consummate professional in every sense of those words. Thank you, Adrienne, for the opportunity to work with you and the fine team at AMACOM. A special thanks to Barbara Horowitz for another fine effort of shepherding one of my books through the publishing process.

Although they were not involved directly in this project, I want to express my appreciation to a number of people who have—through their thoughts, ideas, writings, encouragement, passion, example, sharing of mistakes, humor, or opening my eyes to new directions—been a positive part of my life over the past several years. They include Vince Amen, Steve Bangert, Warren Bennis, Beverly Bensing, Lee Bolman, Tim Buzan, Nancy Campbell, Margaret Carney, Duane Daugherty, John DeGarmo, Emi Dieleman, Steve Ferris, Jim Fetters, Suzanne Frisse, Howard Gardner, Daniel Goleman, Don Hancock, Rick Head, Brian Healy, Charlie Hedges, Frederick Holmes, Miles Hutchinson, Paul Johnson, Ralph Johnson, Hank Kennedy, Matthew Kiernan, Michele Klingler, Phillip Lewis, Linda Light, Sara Lingle, Hunter Lott, Gordon MacDonald, Kay McClure, Sheryl McAtee, Glenn McKee, Barry Minkin, Thomas Moore, Max Muller, Ed Oakley, Cedric Oliver, J. I. Packer, Scott Peck, Tom Peters, Lori Royal, Andy Rowe, Hanna Sano, Shawn Scheffler, Gerry Share, Cindy Sherwood, Ruth St. Pierre, Cyndi Swall, Noe Tabares, Robert Townsend, Barbara Tuchman, Adrian Ulsh, Sara Valins, Bill Walsh, Jeff Weber, Mary Weber, Darby Wiseman, Sandra Young-White and Alex Zaks. There are others, and I know I will be sorry I didn't include you. Please forgive any omissions.

Finally, my thanks to B. D. for all your inspiration and encouragement.

Introduction

The measure of a man is what he does with power.

—Pittacus, one of the Seven
Wise Men of ancient Greece
and ruler of Mytilene, who
voluntarily resigned power
in 579 B.C.

Which is it? Theory "X" or Theory "Y"? Tough-minded leadership or a kinder, gentler variety? Take authority or give authority? I'm in charge or you're in charge? Carry your own load or let me give you a hand?

Should we lead, manage, plan, organize, direct, control, command, and take responsibility? Or should we coach, facilitate, collaborate, involve, listen, advise, serve, and give responsibility?

The organizational world has been bombarded for decades with books that argue one or the other of these positions, *both of which are right*. But these theories lead to peak performance only when taken together in balance. One or the other won't work, at least not at the high levels of achievement required by today's hypercompetitive economy. Organizations that have both but lean heavily to one side or the other will also be less than they could be.

The answer? A balance of power, based on an organization-wide implementation of interdependence and power allocation.

Who Needs This Book?

An important point should be made before we dig in. This book isn't addressed to your organization; it's addressed to *you*. Power doesn't exist in a vacuum, and its application doesn't either. Power transactions are occurring in your life and career right now.

If you have any kind of organizational authority, you are trying to cope with the following questions on an almost daily basis:

> "To whom will I give this assignment? Who should lead the latest project? Who should be put on that team? What do I do with this person who waits to be told what to do? And what about this other person, who never waits before he does things? How can I get this constructive person to accept and release more power? Should I disempower that person, and if so, how do I go about it?"

Real people. Real problems. Real world. Your world.

That's what this book is about and why you need it.

You may have been abused by powerful people. You've seen power used to destroy decent people and good plans for the pettiest and most self-centered of reasons. You've seen some people use power to build lumbering departmental empires, while others use theirs to divide collaborative efforts and sterilize teams. And you may have seen a few people use power well—perhaps as a mentor, an effective team leader, or a visionary near the top of the organizational chart.

This book should connect immediately with you if you know instinctively that the proper sharing and allocation of power are crucial elements in an effective and satisfying organizational life.

Balance of Power is for the leader who is tired of losing control and taking the heat of criticism when subordinates drop the ball, but who is equally tired of taking control and losing the heat of passion when subordinates won't take the ball. It is for the leader concerned about developing his leadership style and skills, the leader who wants to know more about leading individuals, departments, divisions, entire enterprises, and her own career, and the leader who wants to know how to properly handle and share power.

What Is a Balance of Power?

Power is a fabulous thing. And power is a terrible thing.

Nothing—good or bad—gets down without power.

What is power? Power is a force that moves things from one point or state to another.

Power is what allows us to get what we want and to prevent what we don't want. Power means getting results, which are the best measurement of the degree of power involved. Nothing of value—and nothing of horror—gets done without power.

Some power stems from random previous growth patterns or, probably less frequently, from intelligent organizational design (such as positions, titles, charters, mandates), while other power lies latent within the actual people, relationships, teams, and networks that make up the organization. (By the way, the word *organization* in this book doesn't just mean "large enterprise" or overall organization, although those meanings are certainly included; rather, it means "whatever part of the overall organization—group, team, department, division, or the whole thing—for which you are responsible.")

We're going to look deeply into the nature of power, both as a concept and as a hands-on tool of gigantic proportions. We're going to bypass the "my way or the highway" approach, the monopolizing of power by those in authority to the detriment of the organization. And we're going to bypass the "our people are our most important resource" approach as well—because sometimes we don't believe this even though we say it, and sometimes certain of our people are our most important pain in the neck.

Power is a force, and it works to the organization's long-term best interests only when it is accumulated slowly, handled carefully, shared shrewdly, and withdrawn appropriately. The sudden, easy rise to too much power can lead to pride and delusions of adequacy. Power accumulated for personal agendas almost always works to the detriment of the organization (for example, CEOs who move in, take their "cut," and then move on, leaving a bleeding corpse behind) and often to the ultimate destruction of the individual wielding the power (as Julius Caesar, Napoleon, and Hitler found out). Power shared too trustingly leads to the absorption of power by those who are seeking it—often the very worst of candidates.

To be maximally effective, power needs to be balanced—not too much for me, not too much for you. None of us is that trustworthy, and none of us is that wise. It's true that some incredibly powerful people have used their wealth for philanthropy (John D. Rockefeller, for example), but as often as not they built their wealth in the first place on the pillaging of others. To evaluate power accurately, we have to look not only at its ends—its results (Did something get done? Did it add value to our stakeholders? Would we have been better off *not* exercising power?)—but also at its means—its methods (How did it get done? What were the motives of those who did it? Did the action produce any collateral damage?)

Given human nature and marketplace realities, only a balance of power can possibly redeem the use of power in changing the face, the direction, and sometimes even the nature of an organization. And may we be protected from anyone and everyone who has a "mandate," a clear and unobstructed path to power. That is an enticing formula for its abuse.

When we look closely at power and its use, we see that there are two predominant threads: finding the right *quantity* of power for each player through development of well-understood, flexible interdependence; and achieving the right *quality* of power through intelligent, shifting power allocation.

Interdependence and power allocation are the two keys to success in the lean, self-correcting organization of the twenty-first century. In this book, we're going to look at how that balance of power can be found.

This Book and Other Books

You have possibly seen a range of books and articles heralding the advantages of authoritarian management on the one hand

and the empowerment of workers on the other. If you've been in the business world for a number of years, you've seen failures in both directions and understand that the mishandling of power is somehow at the core of the problem.

On the authority side of the argument, there is a long history reaching back to the "scientific management" days of Frederick Taylor. Hal Geneen's *Managing* made a strong case for authoritarian management. The most recent example of this line of thinking is Albert "Chainsaw" Dunlap's *Mean Business*. Much of this "power at and from the top" school of thought is based on models from the military and large church organizations in which thinking is done at the top and orders are followed everywhere else. People like Geneen and Dunlap get much of their credibility from the fact that they have taken over organizations that were "soft" or failing—often because empowerment (at least in the perverted sense of people "doing their own thing") hadn't been countered by intelligent interdependence for years. Other books of this ilk are Anthony Jay's *Management and Machiavelli* and Wes Robert's *Leadership Secrets of Attila the Hun*.

On the empowerment side of the issue, the list is a bit shorter. Robert Townsend's *Up the Organization* was a milestone in the early 1970s. He spoke of empowerment both as giving people freedom and as removing obstacles that would keep them from success. The real guru of empowerment is Tom Peters, starting with *In Search of Excellence*. Many of the companies he discussed in that landmark book have since disappeared (People Express, for example), in part because they had empowerment without interdependence (and related accountability). Peters has continued to advance the empowerment side of the equation with *A Passion for Excellence, Thriving on Chaos, Liberation Management,* and *The Pursuit of "Wow."*

Stephen Covey attempted to bridge the gap in *Principle-Centered Leadership*, where he argued that "tough" management and "kind" management should be transcended by a third alternative that is both tougher and kinder.

But what about the nature of the dilemma between "tough" and "kind" management? Why is dependence (often a product of tough management) harmful? Why isn't independence (often a product of kind management) the answer? What are the barri-

ers to developing interdependence, and how can they be overcome in leaders, other individuals, and teams?

Balance of Power takes the "tough" and "kind" management theories (Theory "X" and Theory "Y") that seem at times
contradictory and shows that they only work when put together
like tongue-in-groove paneling. It also explains that our understanding of power and intentions as to its use *determine* our
leadership style. No given leadership style can be successfully
imposed on an organization that has an opposing power orientation (for example, an empowering style in a command-and-
control organization).

Finally, in this book I will be making a clear departure from
traditional and even more recent approaches to explaining the
difference between leadership and management. In my view, a
leader is anyone in a position or role of authority, regardless of
the presence or absence of titles. Everyone who leads others in
any way is a leader. A manager, on the other hand, plans, moni-
tors, and controls specific activities and transactions. From this
perspective, *everyone* is a manager, *but only of their own work
and not of other human beings*. The only true manager is a self-
manager. Attempts to "manage" others, no matter how rigidly
and relentlessly pursued, are shrouded in illusion.

A Brief Outline of the Book

In Section I, we'll be taking a look at the nature of power. We'll
shake ourselves up a bit by looking at some myths of power. And
we'll take an overall look at the two critical aspects of power in
an organizational setting: the quantity and the quality of power.

In Section II, we'll focus on the *quantity* of power—the
amount any person or team should have—in its different possible settings. We'll see how an imbalance in the quantity of power
leads to the deadly extremes of dependence or independence.
We'll analyze the situations that call for us as leaders to retain
power and then we'll try to understand the remarkable upside-
down principle that sharing power actually increases power—
both ours and the organization's—and that yielding it to others
can at times maximize it. In Chapter 8, we'll go into detail about

how to balance these two aspects of sharing power under the guiding principle of interdependence. In Chapters 9 and 10, we'll take a close look at some factors that will work against us and discuss how to overcome them. Balance is difficult to achieve in any area of life; when we're dealing with something dynamic like power, balancing becomes one of the ultimate and most challenging of leadership skills.

In Section III, we'll concentrate on the *quality* of power— the questions of with whom and for what purposes power should be shared. We'll see how power that is shifted in the wrong direction can "cry 'havoc' and loose the dogs of war." We'll talk about who should and who shouldn't be allowed to exercise power. We have some very specific criteria for you to consider when sharing power with individuals and teams. There are really only four purposes for which people can try to claim power: for a cause, which could lead them to trample others on the way; for others, which could cause them to yield too much power; for themselves, which could cause them to accumulate and monopolize too much power; or—the right answer—for a cause, others, *and* themselves. Only this combination will produce constructive power, and we'll spend time throughout the section, and specifically in Chapter 15, on guidelines you can use to achieve it. In Chapters 16 and 17, we'll get very detailed on some factors that can limit constructive power and produce destructive power, and we'll work together on how they can be overcome.

In Section IV, we'll look closely at how these two power issues—its quantity and quality—flow together. We'll see how an imbalance in one can affect the other, and how imbalances in both can shred the organization's chances of success. Some of these things might surprise you. We'll offer some possible antidotes to these interlocking pressures for an imbalance of power. We'll see how limiting these negative interplays actually enhances overall power and redeems power from the sorry uses to which it is so often put. In Chapter 19, we'll look ahead to the impact that six major social trends are likely to have on building and maintaining a balance of power. We'll close the book with a look in Chapter 20 at why doing these things will be so healthy for your organization, now and in the future.

Finding a balance of power is the only way to create good organizations of any kind or size, as Thomas Jefferson reminded us: "It is not by the consolidation, or concentration, of powers but by their distribution that good government is effected."

May our leadership be "good government."

There are a couple of words in this book that you won't find in a dictionary. The first is *illude*, which I introduced in my book *Fatal Illusions: Shredding a Dozen Unrealities That Can Keep Your Organization From Success.* It is my conviction that all organizations are, to one degree or another, reality-impaired. People spend a substantial amount of organizational time operating under or spreading unrealities—in other words, *illuding.* I merely created a word to go with the malady.

The second word is *powershare. Empowerment* is a limp word—often simply a synonym for *delegation* and all too often a disguise for dumping work on people who don't want it and don't believe that any power is involved in the transfer. *Powershare* suggests a transaction between consenting adults and recognizes that everyone brings some power to the table. Although I elaborate in Chapter 1 on why this word was created, I wanted to introduce it here.

Section I

The Force
and the Issues

1

Power: What It Is and How to Use It

The issue is not size, but power, the ability to either bend other entities to one's own will or to remove obstacles to achieving one's goals.

—Eileen Shapiro,
Management Review,
September 1996, p. 61

Christopher had just been given control of the division.

He felt good about the promotion. Very good. Before leaving work that evening, he did a minitouchdown shuffle, then looked around to make sure no one was watching. On the commute home he could feel the energy coursing through him. Images of the new office, the new title, the eyes looking at him with new respect, the "yes, sir's" all caused him to flush with excitement.

He spent several hours that night making an "early strike" list—things he wanted to see happen quickly, initiatives that he wanted to get his people excited about. Reminding himself that he shouldn't spread himself and his new clout too thin, he prioritized the list before going to bed.

Christopher was startled awake about 2:30 A.M. He didn't know why. Then it hit him. "My God," he thought, "they're going to expect me to make some things happen. Fast. Improve the numbers. Create some new directions. Perform. Deliver the goods." An image flashed into his mind of his former colleagues, now his subordinates. They weren't smiling. But they were laughing.

At him.

Christopher rolled back and forth, checking the clock every few minutes. He felt panicky. A vague but overwhelming dread gripped him.

He finally fell asleep about thirty minutes before his alarm was set to go off.

What Is Power?

Power is life.

And power is death.

But, in spite of the number of times it has been declared to be so, information is *not* power. Information can be good or bad, meaningful or trite, accurate or misleading, incomplete or too voluminous to be read or understood. Information can actually *disempower* if it's wrong, only partly true, irrelevant, or overwhelming.

Information can be a *source* of power, leading others to make decisions either good or bad. The first scientific data on rainfall in western Kansas, collected between 1875 and 1880, seemed to validate the notion that rainfall followed the plow. Encouraged by these figures, settlers broke the prairie sod and planted crops. Unfortunately, the data—while accurate—were misleading, for this atypically wet period was not a true indication of the region's climate. In the drought years that followed, thousands of dispirited farmers moved back east while their fields blew away.[1] Information didn't give those farmers power.

Not even knowledge is power. Knowledge—information sorted, classified, tested, proven, and interpreted in a rational, meaningful way—can still be inadequate. Knowledge, like information, is a source of power; but often in organizations it just lies there, underused or misapplied.

Control isn't power, either. Control can be a component of power for good or bad. *But if we equate control with power, we will never be able to share it.* Any threat to our control will seem to diminish our power. We will miss the counter-intuitive truth that we can give up control and *gain* power.

What, then, *is* power?

According to Webster, it is "an ability or faculty . . . [a] controlling influence . . . authority." Many writers on the topic have described it as an ability to make happen what we want to have happen and to prevent the occurrence of what we oppose. And it implies forceful movement, as captured by its use in physics: "the rate at which work is done or energy transmitted."

But all these definitions fall short of the mark, short of the full potential of power in organizational life. They imply that a person has power for the purpose of using it over someone else, which may be true but is also incomplete. There's no sense of the power that resides in every human being and the additional power that comes from the combining of different individuals' power. Perhaps its use in mathematics captures this idea: Power is "the number of times a quantity is multiplied by itself." There is also no sense in those definitions of the morality of power.

An answer to the question "What is power?" that incorporates these frequent omissions might look like this: *Power is a human force for achievement or obstruction that can be used individually or collectively for the constructive good, or the destruction, of other people and organizations.*

The Morality of Power

"Power is ethically neutral," said John W. Gardner, former secretary of the Department of Health, Education, and Welfare. In one sense, this idea is true. If power could exist in a vacuum, it would indeed be neutral. But power doesn't exist in a vacuum; it exists in the hands of real people in real organizations, people who can use it for great achievements or unfathomable destruction. Power *is* theoretically neutral, but it never exists in theory. It exists only in real transactions between real people, which means that its use is always either ethical or unethical.

Power is a lot like sex. "Power is the great aphrodisiac," said former Secretary of State Henry Kissinger. It can be a strong force that can lift us, at least for the moment, out of the ordinary and help us see and feel our true value and potential. It can also be used for bad purposes, like control or outright degradation. There is no "neutral" sex. And there is no neutral power.

We often hear people speak of "powerful nations" and

"powerful organizations," but the reality is that all power resides in, and emanates from, individuals. Nations and organizations with the observable trappings of power—things like military, economic, or marketplace muscle—but without constructively powerful people will in the long run fade from the scene.

How Power Is Exercised

Individuals exercise power—and everyone has power—either to advance or to hinder the goals of the organization, whether that organization is a team, a department, a production facility, a corporation, a not-for-profit service entity, or a nation. They do so in a number of ways:

• *By making decisions.* The power is there, to whatever degree it's been delegated, taken, or assumed, to make important and constructive decisions at the right time. Or, it can be used to make equally important and destructive decisions at the "right" time—when they can derail the organizational train.

• *By delegating decisions.* Only truly strong and confident leaders can wield their power effectively through the decisions made by their people or teams. Weak, insecure leaders use part of their power to control others and hoard the rest of it, depriving it of its capacity to be used constructively. In William Pollard's words, "It is a grave wrong and injustice for a superior to steal the ability to make a decision from a subordinate."[2]

• *By delaying decisions.* The power to wait, to be patient, to hold your fire until the right moment is used too infrequently in organizations. There is great power in patience and inaction. Poor leaders often don't see the value of using power *not* to do something.

• *By supporting decisions.* Only the naive believe that a decision made is a decision implemented. Power is a critical ingredient of implementation, follow-through, and long-term success. Many valuable decisions have been negated by a flow of destructive power into an implementation vacuum.

• *By vetoing decisions.* There are no perfect decisions. But there are some that are real losers. It takes an exercise of power to say no to a bad idea, especially if a consensus has formed in its favor. It can take even more power to sustain a veto if those favoring the idea use their power to resist.

• *By canceling decisions.* The longer a bad decision has been in place and acted on, the more time and money that have been spent on it, the more power it takes to shut it down. This is complicated by the reality that those who made the decision, or supported it, will often use their power to justify and continue it.

Powersharing

For the organization to have any long-term value, it has to put power into the hands of people who want to make wise decisions based on truth and to prevent the spread of crippling illusions. It also has to keep power out of the hands of those who want to use it to enhance their own positions and to prevent the spread of direction-changing truth.

Sharing power in this way is usually called *empowerment*. I have come to hate this word. It has many flaws: First, it implies that we as leaders have some kind of godlike prerogative to "anoint" others for action. Second, it says that all power resides in us anointers until we decide (or condescend) to share some of it with others. Third, it completely overlooks the barriers and obstacles that may exist within the "empowered" (for instance, they don't want power, they don't know what to do with it, they're afraid to use it, they'll use it to advance their own positions, they'll use it to attack us). Fourth, it is blind to the reality that a huge amount of power—perhaps the bulk of it, perhaps the power that will invent our future—actually exists not in us but in the people whom we so pompously propose to "empower." Finally, it leaves no room for its opposite—the real, crucial leadership activity of disempowering the ineffective and unworthy.

I want to suggest a new word: *powersharing*.

I like the word for a number of reasons:

• *Powersharing closely approximates reality.* Everyone brings power to the organization. In traditional hierarchies, those in positions of formal authority often declare themselves to have a monopoly on power. Then they use a portion of their power to keep their followers' inherent power in check or to prevent them from using it altogether. When leaders stop monopolizing power, they begin to open up the vast reservoir of power that already exists.

• *Powersharing implies a fluidity of power that is crucial to our future success.* Power is used where it is needed. I'll use mine to help you. You can use yours to help me. Leaders will sometimes follow and followers will sometimes lead. It suggests a temporary balance of power "as needed" to accomplish agreed-upon, crucial goals.

• *Powersharing sounds like something human beings would do.* Empowerment sounds like jargon from physics or mechanical engineering.

• *The word* powersharing *has in its very construction the idea of mutuality that* empowerment *lacks.* In the terms that linguists use, *empower* is a transitive verb; it can be done to something or someone ("The leader empowered Bob," for example). *Powershare,* on the other hand, is an intransitive verb; it cannot be done to someone; it can be done only *with* the other person ("The leader powershared with Juan"). It forces us to think "with."

• *Finally,* empowering *has always sounded to me like what they do to people in a chair on death row.*

The Leader's Role in Powersharing

When we use the term *powersharing,* we don't mean "I've got all the power, and here's a little piece for you." That approach is the death of initiative and innovation.

We mean, instead, several things:

• *Recognizing power.* We understand that power is not just "granted" by the usually recognized sources: position, knowledge, competence, effort, charisma, or relationships. Power is everywhere. Everyone has power, for good or for ill. Edison invented what earlier civilizations couldn't even imagine. Salk stopped a disease that the countless tears of millions had never affected. Jefferson Davis and Robert E. Lee couldn't stop Lincoln, but John Wilkes Booth did. John F. Kennedy got Nikita Khrushchev and the Soviet Union to back down in the Cuban missile crisis of 1962, but was shattered by the hands of an assassin in 1963. Martin Luther King saw injustice and replaced it with a powerful dream. Another man, with a gun, committed injustice and replaced that dream with a nightmare.

• *Respecting power.* Power is capable of achieving astonishing results, for good or for ill. One person, with vision and integrity, can stir a forlorn group to hope and action, as British Prime Minister Winston Churchill did with his "finest hour" exhortation to a nation that had been battered and demoralized by Hitler's rapid successes in 1940. And one person, with a perverse mission and willingness to manipulate, can destroy a group on the verge of greatness. Many organizations house these sowers of destruction, people who for bad reasons or no reason at all will undercut us, slander us, lie about us, and destroy our ability to lead.

• *Relocating power.* Power needs to be moved around to be maximally effective. Sometimes I need more, sometimes I need less. Sometimes you need more, sometimes you need less. Sometimes I have to yield some of mine to you, sometimes you need to yield some of yours to me. A static view of power is a formula for entrenched bureaucracy—and, at times, for provoking revolution.

• *Rewarding power.* If we believe that everyone has power, then to make our organization effective we have to reward those who call it forth and use it for good ends.

• *Removing power.* If we respect the potentially harmful effects of power, we'll remove it from those people who use it for misdirected or evil ends. We won't delay, because we know that they can destroy us in an afternoon. And if we can't remove the power from the person, then we may have to remove the person or persons from the organization. Some of these people will show the degree of both their individual power and their nastiness through their post-employment slander and litigation.

Powersharing is a multfaceted, ongoing exercise that is the essence of true leadership. It's a critical element of organizational success. And it's very hard to do well.

Reasons to Use Power

"Power . . . is not an end in itself, but is an instrument that must be used toward an end," said former U.S. Ambassador to the United Nations Jeanne J. Kirkpatrick. After we've fought through to a decision to share power, we must then ask, "For what ends?" To obtain the maximum benefit from sharing power, how should it be used?

Using power ethically, efficiently, and effectively is the vision of a truly successful leader. There are five ways to use power that fit in with such a vision.

1. *Power should be used to enhance the understanding and application of the overall vision of the organization.* Vision is relatively easy to talk about, difficult to fully articulate, and really hard to get across and have implemented. This means that a significant amount of power needs to be put into the hands of people who already understand, believe in, and are fighting to live out the vision.

2. *Power should be positioned where it can deliver benefit to customers and other stakeholders.* This may involve placing it in different locations for different organizations within the same industry, in different locations for different industries, and in various locations within a single organization over time. It may mean allocating more power to product development, design, marketing, customer service, or entry-level sales clerks. When customers' needs change, or we become more aware of the subtleties of those needs, we must be willing to reallocate power to get it where the action is.

3. *Power must be placed where it can be used to align the organization's vision, goals, and actions with* reality. Percep-

tion is not reality, and we are destined to be ever more successful the more closely our perceptions align with reality. Power, when it is used to shred our damaging illusions, is operating in one of its most useful roles.[3]

4. *Power should be located where it can anticipate, prepare for, and take advantage of change* (rather than be used to maintain the status quo). Even more, it should be placed where it can be used to *initiate* change. Some of the most important areas in which change initiatives will pay big dividends on an investment of power are where they will help us do what we do faster, with greater agility, and with a more explicit focus. We are at the top of this mountain when we are quickly able to move power to unexpected opportunities.

5. *Power needs to be located where it can germinate.* The easiest thing to do is to put power where it can get immediate results; a portion of power certainly needs to be positioned there. But giving power to the seed—to the new idea that's years away from commercial application, to the great concept that customers won't even recognize for five years, to the wisp of a thought that may evaporate or may *become* the organization ten years down the road—may be the most important powersharing of all. Few even know that it needs to be done. Even fewer are doing it.

When I say that power should be located or positioned to accomplish certain things, I mean it should be associated with a *person*. Departments and divisions don't exercise power; only the people in them do. Powersharing has to be done both freely *and* carefully, for the same reason: The power will be wielded by a human being, the most complex system on the planet.

●

The ability to balance power wisely is usually not on the lists of effective leadership traits, but over time it may be the most important trait of all. In an age of flattening organizations, power is more, not less, of an issue. "Power is more important in modern organizations *because* its use is far more subtle when it is unbundled from authority. In fact, "less hierarchy . . . make[s] the exercise of power vastly *more* important and tougher to do."[4]

Nobody can get it perfect. The ones who get closest will reap the biggest rewards.

Notes

1. Craig Miner, *West of Wichita: Settling the High Plains of Kansas, 1865–1890* (Lawrence, Kans.: University Press of Kansas, 1986), pp. 47–48, 119–131.
2. From "The Leader Who Serves," in *The Leader of the Future: New Visions, Strategies, and Practices for the Next Era*, ed. Frances Hesselbein, Marshall Goldsmith, and Richard Beckhard (San Francisco: Jossey-Bass, 1996), p. 245.
3. For a detailed program to identify and destroy damaging illusions, see my book *Fatal Illusions: Shredding a Dozen Unrealities That Can Keep Your Organization From Success* (New York: AMACOM, 1997).
4. Robert L. Dilenschneider, *On Power* (New York: HarperCollins, 1994), p. 3.

2

The Myths of Power

Of all the little and big forces that subordinate our actions to superior powers it is ideas that hold the most direct and immediate sway.

—James Hillman, *Kinds of Power*, p. 249

There are a number of myths that can easily confuse us and delude us when it comes to the subject of power.

These myths are ideas that have wide currency in our culture, in the marketplace, and in the organizational literature. Our first reaction when we hear these myths challenged might be to defend them, but please don't do that too quickly; breakthroughs in our leadership ability come first from breakthroughs in our thinking patterns, and getting "out of the box."

As Supreme Court Justice Oliver Wendell Holmes said, "Rough work, iconoclasm, but the only way to get at truth."

Why Myths Persist

Why are myths—ideas that have taken on the form of a permanent "story" even though they are untrue—so persistent?

These myths have at least three driving forces:

Culture

Once something gets written about and talked about long enough from a certain perspective, once enough "authorities"

begin to accept and promote the idea, it permeates the culture
and becomes the "accepted" way to think about the topic. It's
almost impossible to overestimate the power of these cultural
models of thought. They can be passed down from generation
to generation, and be enhanced and embellished as they go from
hand to hand.

One myth that has caused continual misdirection and inef-
fectiveness in our legal system, for example, is that a criminal
owes a "debt to society." We've heard it so often that we might
not even think to question its validity. But the reality is that criminals don't owe a debt to *society*; they owe a debt to the people
they have harmed. Once we abandon the myth and embrace
truth, we can as a society make appropriate decisions. Instead of
"punishing" a thief by making him or her "serve time" and pay
a "debt to society," we can take steps to have the thief pay back
those from whom he has stolen, perhaps in appropriate preset
multiples that recognize the peripheral or long-term losses of the
victim. (A violent thief, of course, presents a separate problem
and may need to be locked up to prevent harm to others.)

Another culturally accepted myth about the legal system is
the notion that an adversarial system will uncover truth. The assumption is that a plaintiff and defendant, battling, attacking,
and counter-attacking each other in front of a "neutral" referee
(judge) or "impartial" audience (jury) will somehow cause the
truth to bubble to the surface. The reality is that the results often
depend on the judge's dysfunctions, on who hired the best attor-
ney (meaning the most expensive, the nastiest, the most willing
to ignore evidence damaging to his own client, the most willing
to destroy others), on which side does the best job of forming a
sympathetic jury, on the interpersonal actions and reactions of
the jury, and on who does the best job of hiding or discrediting
the truth. It's a sporting event with unclear and changing rules.
It's a great system if the goal is to see who "wins." As a truth-
finding system, though, it has outlived whatever usefulness it
may ever have had, and clearly needs to be restructured.

Organizational Framing

How a topic is first presented and considered in an organization
can become the grid or "frame" from which all thinking on that

idea proceeds. If that idea is fundamentally flawed, it can cause great damage, both in the erroneous decisions it produces and the truth it stymies. When the "frame" also ties in tightly with other illusions, it can produce a real lock on our ability to climb "out of the box."

For example, as Stephanie Coontz points out, the debate over family policy "is often framed in terms of how many 'Ozzie and Harriet' families are left in America"—that is, families with a breadwinner father, homemaker mother, and dependent children.[1] Since only a minority of American families fit this category, the conclusion drawn is that families are in serious trouble, and we need government intervention in one form or another.

But the truth is that Ozzie and Harriet are not indicative of the situation most families faced throughout history. As Coontz points out:

> For every nineteenth-century middle-class family that protected its wife and child within the family circle . . . there was an Irish or a German girl scrubbing floors in that middle-class home, a Welsh boy mining coal to keep the home-baked goodies warm, a black girl doing the family laundry, a black mother and child picking cotton to be made into clothes for the family, and a Jewish or an Italian daughter in a sweatshop making "ladies" dresses or artificial flowers for the family to purchase.[2]

By assuming that the ideal family lived in 1950s suburbia, we skew our ability to think critically about the challenges our society faces. A replacement frame is clearly needed.

Personal Mental Models

Our own preconceived ideas can keep us doing the same thing over and over again, all the while hoping to get a different result. We may "know" something is the right, and perhaps the only, way to do things, and yet be not only wrong but seriously harmed by the results of that thinking.

As employers, we have learned to feel that the only right

answer related to giving references is to say nothing. It's the "smart" thing to do, and certainly the dominant mental model of leaders and human resources professionals at the time of this writing. What it really is, in many cases, though, is the triumph of fear over truth, cooperation, and intelligent decision-making about prospective employees. This mental model will be under increasing attack in the future by litigation charging negligent referral, but it will no doubt take a lot of pain before the model is adjusted.

Some Key Myths About Power
That Sound Like Truths

Let's take a look at some dominant ideas, or illusions, that can misdirect us in dramatic ways.

The Myth of Empowerment

Empowerment, as the concept has generally been taught, isn't a bad idea.

But it isn't a good one, either.

Empowerment is an illusion.

As discussed in Chapter 1, the grandiose concept that we have a hold on all the power and then have the wisdom to grace our employees with it is really an uncalled-for molding of reality. But it's even worse than that: It's bad thinking.

Empowerment is a myth in part because it puts too much responsibility on us (to discover and draw out all the power and capabilities in the people who work for us) and in part because it puts too little demand on the people who work for us (by expecting us to find in them what they should be finding in themselves).

There's a lot of power in our organizations. We have some of it, and everyone else has some of it, too. We probably have less than we think we do, and they probably have more than we think they do.

Our power, and the decisions and initiatives that flow from it, can be negated by the overt and covert actions of employees who are theoretically disempowered. Even the power we choose to "share" with them can be canceled by their unwillingness to use it for the good of the organization.

Their power can be used for negative or destructive ends. And they can choose to disempower themselves by not using the power where it can do some good, by not approaching problems with freshness and creativity, by simply using only a small fraction of their abilities on our behalf.

The power is here, and the power is there. Drawing on it, balancing it, and using it for constructive purposes are the most we can hope to accomplish.

Self-empowerment is the only kind that's real. Everything else is powersharing.

The Myth of Motivation

We don't have the power to motivate anyone.

Motivation, as a useful concept, has become pure myth. The idea that we have the power to motivate complex human beings to do what we want consistently and effectively is illusion.

But illusion sells. Countless books and tapes and seminars are ready to give us the million and one ways to ring the Pavlovian bell and create a "correct" response. We just need to find the "right" brew.

But there is no right brew. There are no tricks. What might stir Susan is a turnoff to Bill and becomes an entitlement to Joanne.

The most we can hope to do is to create an environment where people can choose to be motivated—*self*-motivated. An old piece of wisdom says that "the door to change is opened from the inside." We have the power to knock on the door.

But only the one on the inside has the power to open it.

The Myth of Control

We all love to be in control.

And we never will be.

Control is at one and the same time seductively alluring and exasperatingly elusive.

We have a tightly packed daily schedule. Everything is work-ing, everything connecting, we're making progress and feeling successful. Then at lunch the service is slow and our schedule is blown. Or an important customer calls with a major and surpris-ing complaint. Or a key employee gives notice. Poof! Our control is gone.

Or, more accurately, it was always only an illusion.

Nicholas I, Czar of Russia, understood this when he said, "I don't rule Russia; ten thousand clerks do." The hundreds or thousands of decisions and comments and interactions that occur every day in our organizations are hopelessly uncontrolla-ble by us. Even expert micromanagers in small businesses can't do it. They think they've got all the holes plugged up and— whammo!

It's those *people.* They just can't be controlled. They just *won't* be controlled. The stronger the attempts to do so, the more the resentment grows—and the greater the ingenuity. Peo-ple can be incredibly creative in slipping out of our grasp—or in deceiving us into thinking they're in it. "To do nothing is in every man's power," said Dr. Samuel Johnson.

Systems of control. We can talk about them as though they might really work. Dictatorships with secret police willing to shoot people have tried "systems of control." Something deep inside human nature laughs at the concept. Little children are living proof that control is a myth. How can we control an organi-zation when we can't control a five-year old?

The most we can ask for, expect, and base our powersharing on is self-control. If present and nurtured, it is enough.

The Myth of Loyalty

We hope for it. We long for it. We ask for it. We plead for it. We might try to buy it with just the right package of benefits.

And then we just don't get it.

Loyalty is a complex response. If someone is really loyal, it is generally to a specific person. It can involve appreciation, re-spect, gratitude, patronage, and even love. If the truth be told, it doesn't happen to us very often in a lifetime.

Some give their loyalty to the "organization," a faceless object of allegiance. Some of these people—probably more today than ever before—find that their loyalty was severely misplaced, as the leadership mix changes or the organization shifts form and downsizing begins.

People and organizations change so often and in so many ways that loyalty becomes an impossible goal to achieve by strategy or formula throughout an organization.

This is further compounded by the fact that much of what is thought to be loyalty is really just inertia or dependency. And much of what is thought to be disloyalty, such as disagreement, insistence that a solitary opinion may be right and that everybody else might be wrong, may be the closest thing to loyalty that organizations ever see.

If we base our powersharing on hopes that other people will be loyal or that our powersharing will *produce* loyalty, we're proceeding from some very shaky premises. If we powershare intelligently, we can hope for—even expect—commitment to *this* vision, *this* strategy, *this* goal. *Today*. Anything else is illusion.

I am loyal to a few people. A few people are loyal to me. It's a strong statement of relationship, and a true blessing. No organization could hope to ask for this gift.

Or to get it, if it does ask.

The Myth of Boundaryless Organizations

The wave of the future.

We're so interconnected, open, and reasonable that we can be "boundaryless." We can't tell where our organization ends and yours begins.

When individuals are boundaryless, they're considered by psychologists to be relationally dysfunctional. If I don't know where I end and you begin, then I don't know how (or don't have the emotional strength or will) to set and maintain my own priorities and goals, to make my own decisions, to say a firm no or a truly willing yes. I don't become connected to the other person, as two strong individuals in a mutually supportive relationship are, but rather become enmeshed in a confusing, life-draining dance of emotional death.

Setting boundaries becomes a large first step in attaining health of mind and relationships. The same is true for organizations. An organization with strong, healthy boundaries knows what its mission is and, just as important, what its mission isn't. It won't be misled or de-energized by a weak, clinging partner. It is free to connect where appropriate and to disconnect when necessary.

Boundaries are necessary in order to have a clear and workable powersharing with accountability, both with employees and other organizations. Healthy boundaries aren't walls, designed to keep others away and make relationships difficult. On the contrary, they're needed to make all players in a relationship, and thus the relationship itself, strong.

Rich, multifaceted relationships between strong organizations, yes. But no confusion or enmeshment. Boundaries—fences, not walls—are crucial to an effective use of power.

The Myth of Management

This may be the hardest one to swallow.

Management is a myth? How can management be a myth? I'm a manager, for goodness sake. It's in my *title*.

The very word *manage* means "to exercise control over; to handle, manipulate; to influence (someone) so that he does as one wishes." It implies that we have control, that we have the power to order events and ensure their proper occurrence.

Could anything be further from the truth? All business interactions are transactional, which means they involve at least two people. Only the people actually involved in the transaction can truly manage it. "The leader who tries to know it all and to tell everyone what to do is doomed to failure. The leader who believes that there is only one best way and attempts to write detailed procedures has no chance."[3]

Management hasn't always been a myth, but it has become one in the postindustrial, information-and-knowledge age in which we're living. The most tyrannical control freak can't be present at all the interactions with customers, can't find most of the ways to streamline operations, can't stay on top of all the new knowledge and information, and, most important, can't make people be creative—which is the 90 percent of what they're capable of doing that's *not* in their job description. Today, even if we wanted to manage people's jobs, we still wouldn't have the time to pull it off.

Much has been said in the literature over the years about the difference between leadership and management. Part of the problem is that we look at this as two things we do related to other people. The reality is that we lead others, but can manage only ourselves. As we will see in Chapter 8, the ultimate difference between leadership and management is the difference between what we *can* do related to others and what we *should* do related to ourselves.

We have the power to lead—to establish a vision, to articulate plans and goals, to use the power of example. We have the power to do the right thing. And we have the power to recognize the limitations on our ability to manage anyone or anything and to take steps in accordance with that reality. We can create an environment where people can and will, by and large, manage themselves.

Self-management is the only real management. It begins with having something worth working for and being properly "matched" (that is, having the appropriate values, interests, and abilities) with what we're being asked to do. Leadership means leading people into a position to succeed as *self*-managers.

When we try to exercise a power to manage, it too easily transforms itself into a power to obstruct, a power to irritate, a power to slow down.

Everyone who works for us is a manager, a self-manager. We can lead them if we're wise, use our power carefully, and know its limitations. But "manage" them in the world we're living in today? Pure illusion.

Laying Aside the Myths

As we dig into this crucial subject of power, we have to approach it with two ideas in tension.

The first is that power is the driving force behind anything that gets done, whether good or bad. Power is an awesome tool.

The second is that power can't do what power can't do. Power is a limited tool.

Only when we see both sides—that power is awesome and that power is limited—can we succeed in balancing it in our organizations.

Notes

1. Stephanie Coontz, *The Way We Never Were: American Families and the Nostalgia Trap* (New York: BasicBooks, 1992), p. 24.
2. Ibid., pp. 11–12.
3. Marshall Goldsmith, "Ask, Learn, Follow-up, and Grow," in *The Leader of the Future: New Visions, Strategies, and Practices for the Next Era*, ed. Frances Hesselbein, Marshall Goldsmith, and Richard Beckhard (San Francisco: Jossey-Bass, 1996), p. 236.

3

The Quantity and the Quality of Power

Greatness lies not in being strong, but in the right use of strength.

—Abolitionist Henry Ward
Beecher

Sylvia was stunned.

"Could you . . . try that again?" she asked weakly.

Tom shifted in his chair, lifted up the top paper in front of him to scan something underneath, and leaned back. "Let me say it this way, Sylvia. Your department is out of control."

"I . . . I don't understand."

"I know. That's part of the problem. The department's productivity has trailed way off. You've got committees and teams proliferating every which way. They're producing high-quality analysis and reports, but too few and too slowly to make a significant contribution."

Sylvia felt panicky. "I believe in powersharing," she replied nervously. "I just want to get everyone involved."

Tom leaned forward and laid his arms on the desk. "I have to be honest with you, Sylvia. It seems to me that what 'powersharing' means to you is that other people will do and decide everything."

"I still don't . . . under . . . ," her voice cracked and she stopped.

"Sylvia, where is individual *responsibility? Where is indi-*

*vidual accountability? Every decision in your department is by
consensus. Every action is taken by a group. In the first place,
it's terribly inefficient. In the second place, no one feels responsible for any mistakes or problems. Nobody feels it's his or her
job—individually—to improve things."* He paused. *"Frankly, I
think that includes you."*

Sylvia was upset. *"I take my job very seriously."*

He nodded. *"I know you do. Dedication isn't the issue here.
It's the place of the individual versus the group. My definition
of 'powersharing' has room for both individual and team applications. And it starts with the leader. It starts with the person
in charge realizing that she'll need to do some things through
groups, some through individuals, and some on her own. In
short, I believe that powersharing is a multifaceted, organizationwide concept."*

Back to school, *Sylvia thought.*

"One more thing," Tom said. *"A few of the people you've
got out there shouldn't, in my opinion, have any power. Mark
and Stephen—I'm not sure they're really with us. Mark looks
hyperpolitical to me. I think he'll use any power you give him
to advance himself. And Stephen looks for all the world like
he'd use any power he had to cover up his mistakes and to
delegate blame."*

"Give power to some but not others?"

"Exactly," Tom agreed. *"And it needs to happen now."*

Power and Interdependence

The application of power always produces one of three organizational realities: dependence, independence, or interdependence.

If we share too little power, we'll produce dependence in
our followers, which cripples individual performance and initiative. They'll wait for orders from "on high," go through the rou-
tines, just "do their job." We'll get 100 percent of their physical
presence, 10 percent of their minds, and 0 percent of their
hearts.

If we share too much power or share it with the wrong people, we'll produce independence in our followers, which cripples team performance and synergy. They'll do things we don't want them to do, when we don't want them to do these things, and use the excess of power (the additional amount beyond what they need) to benefit themselves and build empires. We'll get a lot of their minds and hearts, but have them working in the wrong directions on the wrong things.

Often, dependence and independence exist side by side in organizations, crippling them in *all* directions. Some people do nothing, while others do the horrible. Dependent employees and teams drain energy and stifle creativity. Independent employees and teams destroy trust and kill collaboration. Dependence leads to inaction and bureaucracy. Independence leads to chaos and anarchy. Both can lead to the organizational cemetery.

But if we avoid these two deadly extremes and share the right amount of power with the right people at the right time, we'll produce intelligent interdependence in our followers. The power can then be used in a collaborative way for many good purposes and few bad ones. They'll need each other, to piece their individual power together, to achieve their goals. This kind of shared power can be used well, and even enjoyed by the users.

Leaders of today have to know when to lead—and when to follow. When to be decision makers and when to be coaches. When to put obstacles in front of their people and when to remove them. When to monitor and when to mentor. When to look closely and when to look the other way. When to show the way and when to get out of the way.

Leaders of today need people who know when to take charge, make decisions, take risks, set objectives, and change course. Just as much, they need people who know when to stop, ask questions, seek counsel, accept their role, and take orders. And, to complicate matters, these are the same people. Leaders in the twenty-first century desperately need the interdependent employee and team and an organizationwide balance of the quantity of power.

But these things don't come ready-made. Leaders have to have a vision for the interdependent organization, be it a service group, sales force, production operation, division, or entire company. Then leaders have to eliminate the factors that breed both dependence and independence, and introduce the elements that allow interdependence to flourish.

Some have argued that existing organizational interdependence (that is, my success in part depends on you or your part of the organization) creates the need for me to use power intelligently to get things done because I can't accomplish my goals alone.[1] While this is certainly true, it is only a small part of what we're talking about here. In one sense, that definition only deals with getting things done by using influence to bend organizational politics to our advantage (or, more likely, to at least negate the worst effects of organizational politics on our plans and goals).

In this book, we aren't looking at power as a way to manipulate and get around the piecemeal and at times irrational interdependence that already exists. We're proposing the design and maintenance of a powersharing system of interdependence that maximizes the total quantity of power available to the organization.

How Much Power and to Which People?

Interdependence—a true balance of power—requires putting power where it can do the most good and keeping it out of the hands of those who will use it for selfish or destructive ends. There are two questions at the core of a balance of power: First, "How much should be kept and how much should be yielded?" This is a quantity question. Second, "With whom and for what purposes should it be shared?" This is a quality question.

To answer these questions, we as leaders are going to have to adjust our understanding of the nature and allocation of power in several ways. First, we have to fight through our preconceived ideas, fears, illusions, and the masks of our followers to share power at all, much less to share it wisely. This isn't easy, because leadership is often thought of, and even defined, as "a position of power." How can I powershare without diminishing my role? How will this affect my importance to the organization? Haven't I worked hard to get this power?

To fight these fears and illusions, we're going to have to dig down deep into the recesses of our mental models. We're going to have to get past the silly and unhelpful idea that "all people at their core want to take initiative, collaborate, and work for the good of the organization." These Pollyannaish views of people are mental models that will destroy our chance to effectively build an organizational balance of power. And we also have to get past the understandable but untrue idea that "all people at their core want to take advantage of us, do their own thing, and play politics." These cynical views of people are alternate mental models that will also destroy our chance to build an organizational balance of power.

We have to be wary of people, because some *will* respond to our allocation of power by using it as a self-aggrandizing tool or as a lethal weapon. And we have to entrust and ennoble and powershare with people, even though some *will* misuse and abuse it. We have to believe in people, even though it is ridiculous to do so.

Second, we're going to have to help our followers fight through their own preconceived ideas (for example, "I'm here to take orders, not initiative"), fears, illusions, and uncertainties about expectations to effectively utilize shared power. This isn't easy, because the very term "follower" implies trailing behind a person of power. These followers might well be asking: "What advantage to me is there in having more power? Will it be given to me with a lot of strings attached? If I have more power and make a mistake, does it simply mean that I'm in bigger trouble?"

Finally, we will have to understand that there are no "once and for all" answers to the questions of how much power should be shared and with whom. These answers are very much a moving target, and we'll have to learn to be comfortable with the flux.

We encourage someone to try some new ideas. She makes a good try, but fails. We avoid "shooting the messenger." We encourage her to self-empower even more, and make sure she has the tools, such as the proper training, to use her power well.

We encourage someone else, and he goes off on a tangent. He starts using the power he has received to obstruct and veto and negate. We try to redirect him and align him with organizational goals. He persists in using his power to achieve his own agenda. He writes long policy memos and extensive procedure manuals. He makes it hard to do business, with him and in general. We begin to disempower him. We restrict his ability to set up roadblocks and detours.

Some will respond slowly to our powersharing, clinging to their dependence on us to tell them what to do and how to do it. Others will respond quickly, rushing to their newfound freedom to do what they want, the way they want to do it. Some will take whatever quantity of power they have and use it for destructive ends. Some will use small allocations of power properly in an attempt to impress us and get more that can be used for their own purposes or destructively.

A few—a minority, at least at first—will use the right quantity of power necessary in given situations in a generally constructive way. Recognizing this group and channeling power in their direction is the difficult, but absolutely necessary, skill of a truly effective leader.

Note

1. See, for example, Jeffrey Pfeffer's *Managing With Power: Politics and Influence in Organizations* (Boston: Harvard Business School Press, 1992), esp. pp. 38–41 and 66–68.

Section II

The Quantity of Power

4

Dependence and the Death of Initiative

Corporations and other large employers are among the last bastions of dictatorship. Within the more bureaucratic organizations, work life more closely resembles life in a totalitarian state than life in a free nation.

—Gifford and Elizabeth Pinchott, *The Intelligent Organization*, p. xv

"I've been waiting for three months to get that plan approved," moaned Kip.

"Why the wait?" Jeannie asked sympathetically.

"Same old same old. Ten levels of review. Everybody's got to have their chance to rip it to shreds."

Jeannie frowned. "Do you really think that's all those people want to do?"

Kip cradled his coffee cup between his hands. "No, that's not all," he said seriously. "They have a lot to do. It takes a lot of time and thought to position yourself so that you get much of the credit if the idea works and none of the blame if it doesn't. The ones who are really good at this will be able to prove later, if it fails, either that they have never heard of it or that they had concerns about it from the get-go."

"You sound like a cynic."

"I'm not a cynic, Jeannie; I'm a realist. They hire you, theo-

*retically, to do things, and then build structures and spend all
of their time to make sure you can't do them."*

*Jeannie took a bite of her dessert. "Did you at least put a
'drop-dead' date in the report?"*

"A what?"

*"A drop-dead date. You know: 'If I don't hear to the con-
trary by such and such a date, I'm moving ahead.' It allows you
to take some action and still be covered."*

"I tried that once."

"Did they get back to you by your date?"

"No."

"Then did you go ahead?"

He looked at her incredulously. "Are you kidding?"

"You didn't?"

*"No. That's crazy. They would've killed me. I was hoping it
would bring some pressure to bear, but it didn't. If I'd gone
ahead without their approval, though . . . Jeannie, that's what's
called a 'CLM.' "*

"What's a 'CLM'?"

"A career-limiting move."

"So you're just going to wait?"

"Uh-huh. That's why they're paying me the big bucks."

Good Things Don't Come to Those Who Wait

Dependent organizations are characterized by waiting.

Waiting to get permission. Waiting to see what the boss
thinks. Waiting to see what other people say or do. Waiting to
see what gets people into trouble.

Waiting. Withering. Dying.

People wait because they don't have an alternative. The
mere thought of not waiting—of taking some initiative or out-of-
the-ordinary action—seldom or never gets serious consideration
in a culture of dependence. The uncertainty is simply too great.
The fear that tags along with the uncertainty is even greater.

The cost of not waiting is simply too high for the individual.
Criticism, poor performance evaluations, charges of not being a
"team player" (read: mindless puppet), public humiliation, demotions, even terminations await the brave and the bold when

dependence permeates the culture. The cost to the individual of not waiting is, in such a culture, very understandable.

But the cost of waiting is too high for the organization. Unhappy customers, lost sales, missed opportunities, sidetracked innovations, and ideas that never even get suggested dog the culture that's permeated by dependent people.

In a dependent environment, the cost of waiting is for most people preferable to the cost of not waiting, even if this means long-term organizational decline. There have to be strong incentives to get people to stop waiting, but the incentives in a dependent culture are all pointing—no, pushing, pressing—in the opposite direction.

People will wait to be told what to do. They'll hate it. But they'll wait.

The Root of Dependence

It would be easy to say that dependence is created by structure and hierarchy, but the cause goes deeper, into the core of who we are as human beings.

We like to be in control. In truth, we can only control ourselves. But as most of us who have made New Year's resolutions know, self-control is very hard to achieve, given our passions and desires and drives and habits. So we are tempted to skip self-control and move on to the "next best thing" (which is really not a "next best"): We can try to control our environment. But we can't do that, because people keep messing up our perfect plans. So we're led to the logical but illusory conclusion: To control our environment, we have to control people. And to control people, we've somehow got to make them dependent on us.

Then we build structures and hierarchies that support this need to control. They can include "positive" dependency builders, like money, incentives, and approval, or "negative" dependency builders, like fear, insecurity, and disapproval.

Those who have gone before us, perhaps, did the early building, and we add our agreement by our actions. We pay attention to the structure, which in reality is a pyramid, regardless of how "humbly" it is drawn on organization charts. We eye those above us. We do the things that inch us upwards and avoid oh so many things—like initiative, risk taking, constructive criticism, and creative suggestions—that could cause us to fall out of favor.

It's the game, and we learn how to play it. But it's an enervating game, and our organizational life drains out on the floor.

The Forms of Dependent Organizations

All dependent organizations are structured in a top-down, command-and-control, pyramidal manner, although the really insidious ones cleverly draw it as an upside-down pyramid with the CEO at the bottom and customer service people at the top. But the methods that they use to try to exert control vary. Some typical management styles include the following:

The Tyrannical Organization

Charles was president of a family-owned business with 175 employees. He ruled with an iron fist. He made every decision. All mail flowed through his office. No form could be changed without his approval. He abused people verbally for making "stupid" decisions, which meant any decision that he had not personally initiated and overseen.

Yet at the same time he harassed people for "showing no initiative." He—and his father, who was chairman of the board—had managed to create the worst of all possible organizational worlds: employees who were terrified both of taking action and of not taking action. His organization was in reality a dysfunctional family with a business attached to it.

There are billion-dollar organizations that are at core dysfunctional people with thousands of co-dependents (that is, people who support the power addiction of the tyrant). No one can say or do anything except "as approved." Advancement doesn't depend upon achievement but rather upon not rocking the boat or posing a threat to those who have the monopoly on power.

In this kind of environment, people are not in a position to exercise power in any meaningful way. The taking of action is viewed as a usurpation of the power of those at the top. But people will do something with whatever personal power they have. Even while they are dependent and fearful, they will yearn for freedom and independence. They will find those things they yearn for in subtle, guerrilla ways. And if they ever get into a position of formal authority, they will probably become oppressors. "Today's rebel is tomorrow's tyrant," said historians Will and Ariel Durant.

The Paternalistic Organization

Sharon was sure she had a potent new product idea. But when she shared it with Al, he laughed and shook his head.

"It'll never fly," he said, matter-of-factly.

"You don't think it's a good idea?"

"Sharon, it's a terrific idea. If it works, it could open up a whole new line and put us a notch ahead of the market leaders. I love it from a sales perspective because our primary line has become a commodity. All we have to compete on is price. Your idea could break that downward spiral."

Sharon looked puzzled. "Then why don't you think it would fly?"

"Because you're in sales! This company has a highly educated, even higher-paid product development group whose charter is to do new stuff. Worse, you're a newcomer. You haven't been here long enough to be listened to. You haven't earned your stripes."

"You mean they don't even want my opinion?"

Al smiled. "They do. But when they want it, they'll beat it out of you."

"Do they think they know everything?" Sharon asked, frustrated.

"No. They know they know everything."

Paternalistic cultures, based on the "father knows best" idea, are still tyrannical. They're just the kinder, gentler variety.

Paternalistic cultures are characterized by strong "this is the way we do things around here" atmospheres, the "one best way" approach. Information is doled out sparingly on a need-to-know basis as determined by the "father." Feedback from the troops is rarely, if ever, sought (after all, they're just "kids"), and if it is, it is often done in a dishonest way ("We're asking your opinion because the management books say we should, but we're not going to take it seriously because you're not us"). Power is dispensed, very unliberally, with an eyedropper. Often, it's just enough to give people the rope with which to hang themselves as they explore the possibility of doing something in a different way and then get strung up for the trying.

These cultures produce a cadre of people who come to hate the organization but who just can't leave because it feels so good to be "taken care of" (we should *never* want the people who work for us to desire to be "taken care of"). Paternalism leads to sibling rivalry as each person or department vies for the attention, approval, and inheritance of the "father."

This sibling rivalry is almost certain to occur because whenever we create a top-down family structure, we invite its attendant problems. Since relationship to the top of the "family," rather than achievement, is the measure of success, it is very easy for leaders and executives to display the behaviors that produce sibling rivalry (or for our "children" to interpret our actions in this way). These behaviors include showing unfair preference for one over another; withholding benefits and incentives people can legitimately expect (birthrights) and rewards for work well done (approval); permitting the more aggressive to grasp what isn't legitimately theirs and to control those who are less aggressive; intervening in or taking sides in childish squabbles; and practicing total "equality" in our treatment of widely different personalities and competencies.

People often feel isolated, disconnected, and uneasy when they're in the presence of those who hold the power monopoly in this type of culture. A twisted kind of loyalty is demanded— not loyalty to the truth, or to customers, or to organizational success, or to fellow employees, but loyalty to the Grand Duke or Duchess, the patriarch of the "family." In the paternalistic world of colonial Latin America, for example, "Favours were extended in exchange for respect and loyalty; special protection in a harsh world was the reward for obedience."[1] In such a culture, one rises by being a "good child," which usually means doing things the "family way" (even if the "family way" doesn't prepare the organization for the future, even if the "family way" is dysfunctional).

In addition to all its other flaws, the paternalistic organization plays to the negative personal family memories and related dysfunctions of a significant percentage of its employees. There is little difference in practice between an authoritarian, controlling family and an authoritarian, controlling corporation. People can feel crippled by the similarity their first day on the job. Even worse, some may try to recreate and "fix" their family of origin inside the walls of the inviting, paternalistic organization. If you're at the head of the "family," a lot of their "fixing" and inbred expectations will be coming your way.

Families and organizations are similar in many ways. Many, if not most, of the same principles apply. Communication, promises, expectations, forgiveness—all have their necessary place in both types of organizations. In a certain sense, we should at least question the ability of someone to successfully lead an organization if he can't at a minimum learn from his personal failures and apply those lessons to the larger organization. We should at a minimum note that the person's leadership flaws are likely to produce the same results in both places, and prepare to counteract these potential problems. As Tolstoy noted in *Anna Karenina*, happy families are remarkably alike. Healthy organizations also have core similarities, which is why books can be written about the common factors that make organizations effective.

Unfortunately, this similarity is also true of negative, immobilizing structures like paternalism.

The Trick-or-Treat Organization

She glared at those lining each side of the long table. Several people shifted uncomfortably in their chairs. A young man near the far end of the table nervously shuffled some papers.

"Have I made myself clear?" Rachel asked.

Everyone knew Gloria would be the first to speak up. "Rachel, I know we're looking for the same thing—a more highly

*motivated workforce. I'm just not sure that those changes to the
policy manual are going to get us there."*

"Why not?"

*"It's too . . . it's mostly negative stuff. More restrictions on
how people can take time off. More penalties for coming in late.
More. . . ."*

*"I know what's in the manual," Rachel said icily. "Tell me
something I don't know."*

*Gloria looked around for support. All eyes were looking
down at the table. "I just don't see how more restrictions are
going to get people to be more creative and. . . ."*

*"I don't even need them to be creative. I'd be happy if those
people just showed up on time and did what they were told. The
purpose of these changes is to get people off their duffs, to
tighten things up, to make things clear. We're just trying to be
professional. And we've added some incentives for good, on-
time attendance. We can look for creativity down the road."*

"It'll be a long search," Gloria muttered.

"What's that?"

"I agree. We'll look for creativity later."

*Rachel smiled. "I'm glad we're pulling together on this,"
she said.*

In the trick-or-treat, carrot-and-stick organization, we switch
from the dictatorial control of tyranny and the benevolent control of paternalism to the mind-game control of the manipulator.

The "trick" side can come in the form of the "policy and
procedure manual." Long lists of rules, detailed disciplinary
processes, criticism of anything outside the acceptable norm are
all part of this "stick," which is intended to keep people from
getting out of line.

The "treat" side comes in the form of promotions, raises,
cost-of-living allowances, bonuses, profit sharing, and a nice
package of benefits. All this is designed to produce a "carrot"
that will keep people doing it our way.

This is "comfort theory," which is based on the true but less
then ennobling idea that people will work hard to find pleasure
and to avoid pain. It makes people dependent in part because it
treats them like children and in part because it treats them like

laboratory rats. In this culture, people become dependent on the manipulator to give them their treat and not to play tricks on them if they're "good" (with "good" often defined by the manipulator rather than customer needs or marketplace reality).

Interdependent organizations will also have policies, discipline, and financial packages. The difference is that the dependent organization uses these things to enforce *its* will on its dependents, while the interdependent organization uses them to encourage effective decision making and collaboration.

Results of Dependence

Among the many results of a dependence-dominated culture are:

Helplessness. This is the disempowered role of victims who can do nothing to alter their situation. They expect the people at the top to be responsible for them. And they expect nothing ever to change. Since they aren't permitted to have boundaries, they can never say no to demands from the top, no matter how absurd or unachievable those demands might be.

Irresponsibility. Over time, dependent individuals can become very irresponsible. This means that they're not willing (or even able) to take any responsibility that's not written into their job descriptions (which can never fully describe all that is necessary), but it means even more. It means that they become unwilling to take responsibility for anything even when it *is* in their job description. "I'm here because I have to be"; "It all pays the same"; "I just do what I'm told"; "It's not my job to think." Dependent individuals become bodies for hire—corporate prostitutes. They can happily use their dependence as a way of avoiding what they need to do, and it can be hard to get them to think differently. "It is difficult to free fools from the chains they revere," said Voltaire.

Scapegoating. Since they think they are helpless, dependent people can easily conclude that their problems must be caused by someone else or some other team or department. They begin playing the "blame game": "That isn't my fault"; "That isn't my re-

sponsibility"; "They were supposed to take care of that"; "I didn't
have enough help, so . . ."; "If you'll read my job description, it
says clearly that. . . ." They blame others for the difficulties they
face rather than accept appropriate personal responsibility, in part
because they think they have no power to keep negative things
from happening or to accomplish positive goals. Yet, by blaming
others they further disempower themselves and unintentionally
give control of their lives to the very ones they are blaming.

Guilt. If they do take any "unauthorized" action, the "you-
shouldn't-have-done-that" voices take over. In a strongly dependent culture, these will start as internal "conscience" voices even
before the external finger pointers get into the act. When people
are drained of power, they constantly struggle with feelings of
dismay, shame, and stupidity.

Silence. Gut feelings, intuitions, and concerns that could
make a difference to the organization—maybe even save it—are
repressed. This is because the message has been sent that it's
"management's job" to do the thinking, forecasting, and react-
ing. Nothing atrophies faster than insight.

Dread. Fear of criticism, falling out of favor, rejection, and
termination come to pervade people's thinking. The message is
loud and clear: play ball our way or we'll take your meal ticket
away.

Insecurity. People can't trust others because they're all competitors for the "father's" attention. Change is especially terrifying because it upsets the fragile family structure.

Procrastination. At any given point in the process, people
can become uncomfortable taking a step if it requires any origi-
nality. "Anything worth knowing, management will tell us" is the
operative philosophy here. In the absence of a clear directive
from "on high," guessing about what management will find acceptable seems too dangerous to those who yearn for approval.
All progress is slow and easily stopped as people wait for crumbs
of information to drop off management's table.

Impulsiveness. Perhaps surprisingly, dependent cultures
produce random, ill-considered acts as people in frustration attempt to break out of their chains. Some of the worst, most
mindless decisions can come out of dependency.

Complaining. Lack of power induces people to give up hope of making a significant difference—or even a significant contribution. People still see the problems, but their hesitancy to think, to be creative and resourceful, to try anything new leads them to conclude that there is no way to alter the situation even slightly. This feeling that they're "stuck" in the situation inevitably leads to grumbling and whining.

Resentment. Ironically, many dependents come to resent their dependency. They don't want to give it up, really, but they aren't happy about it either. They want to have their cake (to be dependent) and eat it (devour us) too. They want to be serfs and they want to be free. They can't have both, but that won't stop them from being angry and hateful about it.

Revenge. Some, here or there, will take their resentment a step further and exact a toll on us or the organization. "Employees in America," claims Jennifer Fuller, "are spreading lies about co-workers, sabotaging assembly lines, and . . . secretly recording the damaging dialogue of fellow executives . . . it's workplace revenge by the disenfranchised against those who control corporate America, to get even for real and perceived wrongs."[2]

The great irony is that the dependents in a disabling culture will be the least prepared for market changes, but will be the first to be laid off en masse. This culture promises protection in return for servitude, but it often delivers only heartache.

Dependent Definitions

In a dependent organization, *initative* and *collaboration* are redefined.

Initiative, rather than meaning taking intelligent risks and exhibiting courage, means "occasionally asking for permission to do something differently."[3]

Collaboration, which at its best means the mutual and supportive effort of interdependent people working toward a shared vision or goal, becomes "following the party line," "working with the system," and "doing what you're told without asking a lot of fool questions."

The Death of Dependence

The result of these redefinitions and the way they play out in day-to-day organizational life is a collective depression that leads to even more dependence. The structure that controls people drains their life and energy so that they become even less able to think or do anything for themselves.

Those in formal authority are almost guaranteed to become angry and hateful and resentful in turn. We've created or allowed this dependency culture to flourish, but no matter—we're sick of all this irresponsibility and mindless going through the motions. We want these people to "get on the ball." We give them lectures about "taking initiative" and "pulling their weight," but it doesn't do any good, because all the cultural, structural, and psychological incentives favor dependency.

Eventually, this culture of dependency will also affect us in a deep and personal way. We'll be carrying so much of the load that burnout can be only a heartbeat (or heart attack) away. And trying to live up to the expectations of so many hungry mouths can leave us feeling like failures, no matter how much we try to give them.

Dependency cultures are a dead end for everyone involved. For most of us, nobody pays our bills, decides where we ought to live, or chooses what we ought to eat or wear. So why do we need this demeaning environment in our work lives?

Yet, like a dysfunctional family, we all become ever more reluctant to talk about the real issues, ever less able to express our concerns, and incapable of trusting those above us and around us. It's a dead end.

But there is a way out.

Notes

1. Edwin Williamson, *The Penguin History of Latin America* (London: Penguin Books, 1992), pp. 146–147.
2. Jennifer Mann Fuller, "The Art of Getting Even," *Kansas City Star,* 26 November 1996, p. A-1.
3. Gifford and Elizabeth Pinchot, *The Intelligent Organization* (San Francisco: Berrett-Koehler Publishers, 1996), p. xv.

5

Independence and the Death of Collaboration

In our age, independence and the ability to get things done are often mutually exclusive.

—Robert L. Dilenschneider,
On Power, p. 13

The Declaration of Independence.

It has such a nice ring to it. People fought and died for it. Its opening words are read, memorized, and quoted around the globe. We understand, instinctively, why people are willing to fight and die for independence—and why nobody would die for a declaration of *dependence*.

And yet, at some level, dependence is not such a bad thing. Babies and small children are obviously dependent on someone—if fortunate, someone who is decent, reliable, and willing to help the child grow *out* of dependence. To a lesser degree, the same is true for people in their first jobs or people who are new to an organization. They don't know how to do some of the fundamental activities (like making contacts, learning the network, and making appropriate recommendations) that lead to success in the organizational culture. Someone has to show them. They need a sponsor or mentor. Until they can do it on their own, they are necessarily and rightfully dependent.

The obvious long-term goal? It *appears* to be independence. Do it on their own. Grow up. Pull their own weight. In a family, we talk about "pushing them out of the nest." In an organization, we talk about people needing to "take responsibility for themselves."

But if we think this way, we're wrong. Independence is not the logical and necessary conclusion to a timely move away from dependence. In a very real way, it is a pendulum swing to the opposite extreme, from "you need me desperately" to "you don't need me at all." But there's a better point to stop at on the "swing."

Interdependence.

If we define independence as "freedom from slavery, bondage, or oppression," then independence is, of course, very good, something worth fighting and dying for. But if we define it as "freedom from restraint, freedom to do what we want regardless of the consequences or the impact on others, freedom not to collaborate," then independence can be very bad, causing fights and organizational death.

Independence is different from initiative.

People who like to be "in control" fail to see this difference. *Somebody takes initiative, she's being independent (and perhaps rebellious). She needs to be reeled in. Boxed in. Put in her place.* The assault on apparent independence becomes the annihilation of initiative.

People who don't understand power, including its destructive form, also fail to see the difference. *Somebody is making her own decisions. That's good. She's showing some spunk.* But it isn't good if those decisions are for her own goals at the expense of the organization's.

Independence at its core is initiative without collaboration.

Unless we're controlling-type personalities or believe that people are totally depraved, we want our people to take initiative. We want them to do the right thing, even when it isn't in the policy manual, even when it's *contrary* to the policy manual. We want them to learn from the mistakes of the past, to have a retention of experience that lets them take the right steps in the present. We want them to take excellent and creative actions in the present on behalf of our customers and our organization. And we want them to live in the future, to make suggestions about what directions we ought to take, and to make decisions today that will make tomorrow livable and profitable.

Initiative is indispensable to success in a rapidly changing, knowledge-based world. We've got to have it or we won't have anything. But the initiative has to find its way in a spirit and framework of collaboration, of working for the common good, of steering in the same direction (provided it's a good one) as the other cars on our organizational highway.

The alternative is a forty-car pileup and death.

Causes of Independence

The primary cause of independence is excess.

In individuals, this can be an excess of confidence in our own abilities, a foolish belief that we can "go it alone" and accomplish more by ourselves than is really possible. In a society laden with motivational speakers, permeated by "possibility thinking," and enamored of personal rights, the degree of this excess can be phenomenal. There are people walking around whose opinion of their abilities bears no resemblance to what they are actually capable of doing. Their "independence" is based on a truly shaky foundation.

We can also have an excess of a desire to be in control. Beyond self-control (which is, by itself, a challenge of a lifetime for most of us), control of other people or situations is largely illusory. Over time, it is always a myth. Attempting to control what can't be controlled leads an organization to be, in consultant Warren Bennis's expression, "overmanaged and underled." It is also a violation of the golden rule—we don't want to be under anyone else's control, but we deny the same privilege to others. This desire to control can make others dependent even as it pushes the controlling person toward independence of restraint. Ironically, this excess of control can also produce independence in others, for two reasons: first, people will be driven to throw off their shackles; and second, people will want the same independence that we're displaying by our example.

Individual excess can also take the form of greed; it is amazing how often greed and the desire to control come as a package. Greed (an excess of ambition) and its corollaries of jealousy (an excess of ownership) and envy (an excess of competition) can lead to the desire to throw off or destroy any connections to others that we perceive as standing in the way of our goals. An incredible amount of power is used to supply energy to greed.

One of the most common examples is the supervisor who constantly preaches and carefully enforces a strict chain of command, watching like a hawk lest anyone below be noticed by anyone above. Another is the administrator who insists that all information, reports, recommendations—anything that represents his area, especially if it makes his area look good—go across his desk and receive his approval (meaning let him get the credit). In both cases, we have an excess of desire to be in control driven by a greed for recognition. This makes managers both very possessive about "their" area and very watchful of any would-be competitors among their subordinates.

In organizations, independence-breeding excess ironically takes two forms: an excess of power *and* an excess of limitations on power.

An excess of power can mean that people are granted more power than they need to accomplish their legitimate goals. The excess can't be stored; organizational power can't be saved up, but has to be used fairly quickly or it's gone. And used it will be. The excess will be applied to personal goals, which can range from the relatively harmless (like making contacts for future employment) to the organizationally disastrous (like building empires, waging turf wars, and playing politics). Given human nature, an excess of power will almost always be used to amplify the self or deconstruct the organization.

This excess of power can also mean that people are granted as much power as they need but more than they can handle. When we allot more power than the maturity level of the person is capable of absorbing and using effectively, the excess, the unabsorbed portion, will once again be used for distracting or nefarious purposes.

We can also produce unhealthy independence by an excess of limitations on power. Independence, in the form of rebellion or revolution, can be kicked into high gear by micromanagement, lists of rules, and a culture of disempowerment. Most people have to have some sense of personal power—at the very least, control of their immediate environment—just to live. An excess of restrictions will always produce at least some personal "declarations of independence."

At the same time, the very excess of limitations that produces independence in some people will produce dependence in others. Power exercised as control always pushes people to these extremes of response because it demands so much (usually so much more than is necessary). Some people, trained by their upbringing and experience to be passive, will lean toward dependence when under the demands and pressure of control. Others, trained to be active in their response, will move toward independence.

Control is a sorry excuse for leadership and produces both dependence and independence.

And makes interdependence impossible.

The Forms of Independent Organizations

Independence thrives in certain types of organizations. Among these are the following:

The Anarchical Organization

"How did you come up with that price?" Jason shook his head in wonder as he studied the numbers on the screen.

"Simple," Cal said as he scrolled to the next screen. "I lower the price until revenues hit my goal. At some price, you can hit any level of sales you want to. How do you think I win all those sales awards?"

Jason was truly shocked. "I've been playing by the book, and my revenues have been stagnant, just lying there."

"What book have you been playing by?" Cal asked smugly.

"You know. The memo that came out at the end of last year about volume discounts and flexible pricing."

Cal laughed. "My God," he snickered, "you're really trying to follow that nonsense?"

Jason felt foolish. "It just seemed like the right thing to do," he offered lamely.

Cal sat up straight in his chair, turned off the screen, and

*looked up at Jason. "In this organization, the right thing to do
is what benefits you."*

"How do you get that pricing through?"

*"It's all a matter of how you package the numbers. Spread
the deliveries out in varying quantities, never show the discounts as a separate line item, vary the terms with each ship-
ment, slip in overshipments as a 'bonus,' delay sending in the
paperwork until the end-of-month insanity."*

"And they go for it?" Jason was truly impressed.

*"Are you kidding? They just crunch the numbers. They have
no idea what the numbers ought to be, what their costs are, or
which customers are making or losing them money. The only
time I got challenged was when I was under the gun and they
offered to help me put some numbers together. Never again.
Have you heard that slogan, 'It's easier to ask forgiveness than
it is to ask permission'?"*

"Yes."

*"Well, around here it's easier to do as you please than it is
to do as* they *please."*

Jason knew exactly what he'd do on his next proposal.

An anarchy is the formless form of organization. In organizations with weak or absent leadership, or with no clear and compelling vision, people are virtually invited to set their own
agendas, which may have nothing to do with marketplace realities and the corresponding needs of the organization.

In a tyranny, all power is held at the top. In an anarchy, no
power is held at the top. It is allowed to seep out and disperse.
At first, this dispersement will be random. But since the total
power of the organization is available to any who will take it, it
will eventually end up in the hands of those who are most willing
to grab it. Almost always, these are the worst people to hold
power. It isn't power that corrupts—it's too much power in the
wrong hands that corrupts.

The difficulties in an anarchical environment can be dramatically compounded if key stakeholders assume that people will
generally do "the right thing." Without direction and a balance
of power in the organization, we should lay our naïveté aside
and assume that people will generally do the *wrong* thing—the

thing we don't want done—whether that wrong thing is simply worthless or downright destructive.

At its worst, this lawlessness, with all people doing what's right in their own eyes, operates with a secret power. Agendas are hidden. Motives are disguised. People feign loyalty and a willingness to cooperate. But all the while, the subtle power of lawlessness is chipping away at the integrity of the organization.

And yet, even while people are running wild, something in them will yearn for control and order. It's very hard to live at the extremes. Like children from a home without personal boundaries who grow up to be control freaks with their own children, employees who are allowed to run wild can become supervisors who rule with an iron fist in their own impoverished little domains. Those under them can also grow tired of the chaos that comes from not having anyone in charge, so they may become willing to yield themselves to the dictator, the "man on a white horse."

Anarchy leads to a fractionalized entity, akin to the many city-states of ancient Greece or, in later times, the fiercely go-it-alone cities of what is now Italy (in 1814, the Austrian minister Metternich insisted that Italy was "not a nation but a collection of cities"[1]). Too many organizations today are not really organizations, in the sense of being organized around a unifying principle and moving in a common direction, but are instead collections of independent individuals and rogue teams.

The results of the divisions in those pseudo-nations were not positive. The factions exhausted themselves battling for their own little rights and privileges, and because of this exhaustion and their tiny size, stronger forces were able to pick them off.

The results in pseudo-organizations will be the same. While the fiercely independent individuals, departments, and product development groups fight to be on top, the whole is weakened and invites invasion—in the form of heightened competition or, at the extreme, a takeover and dismemberment by outside forces.

The Paternalistic Organization

Paternalism appears both in Chapter 4 and here because it tends to produce both dependence and independence, often existing side by side. We can end up with some people or departments who won't do anything without our blessing, and others who won't do anything we do bless.

The independence responses to paternalism can take at least two forms, open rebellion and subtle resistance.

Some people, often the ones with the most individuality, creativity, and integrity (rare commodities that we desperately need), will resent the stifling atmosphere and openly rebel. The rebellion can take many forms: arguing, fighting, civil disobedience (refusal to support or implement disagreeable plans or policies), and voluntary exile (leaving the organization). The paternalistic culture can rarely tolerate open rebellion for long; rather than looking inward to see what is creating the rebellion, the "fathers" usually choose "tough love" and crack down on the insurgents.

Others, because of personality, background, or experience, will choose the route of quiet resistance. This resistance can take many forms, from passive unhelpfulness (like calling in sick when the pressure is on) to guerrilla warfare (for instance, undercutting management, laughing at company policies, not communicating helpful suggestions, not going the extra mile for customers). This response can, when it reaches a certain level, be frustrating to the "fathers," but they can rarely do anything about it. The structure itself is producing it.

The Political Organization

"I'm not going to lick their boots," Sondra said with disgust.

"If their boots don't shine, they'll kick dirt on ours," Randy responded.

Sondra didn't like the condescending tone in his voice. "To hell with their dirt; let's go ahead without them. The concept stands on its own."

Randy shook his head. "No concept stands on its own."

"You don't think this is a great idea as is?"

"Of course I do. It's a terrific idea. In fact, it may be the best new product idea I've seen in two or three years."

Sondra was flustered. "Then I don't get it."

"I know you don't." He sipped his coffee. "And that's the

problem. You don't get it. Sondra, I'm simply talking about the need to collaborate."

"You mean 'compromise.' "

"Call it what you will. You want a product that would require a whole new set of vendors. With a few changes, our current vendors could do the job."

Sondra shook her head. "Randy, by making those 'few changes' we'll gut what's really original about this product. It won't be any easier for 90 percent of our customers to use, and the maintenance on it will probably go up. It just ends up being nicer to look at with a few more bells and whistles."

"There are powerful forces at work to avoid a massive change in our supply chain," Randy said in a slightly louder tone.

Sondra laid her notebook on the edge of his desk. "You mean the purchasing department."

"It includes them, yes. But there are other things going on here that you just can't see from your vantage point."

"Are those vendors in bed with somebody at the top?"

Randy furrowed his brow. "That's uncalled for."

"What else am I to think?"

"Here's what you need to think. There are two ways to approach this. One, we make the changes, give up a little on some things our customers have never heard of and won't even know are missing, get everybody on board, and you're a hero. Or two, be a hardhead, and I kill the idea here to avoid others killing it later. Your choice. Pretty simple, really."

Résumé time, *Sondra thought as she leaned back in her chair.*

In the political culture, power is transformed into a game, often a very ugly game.

Power in this environment is allocated rather than randomly dispersed, but it's allocated on incorrect principles. Rather than being correctly allocated between leaders and followers on the basis of meeting legitimate needs, it's allocated by fiat according to criteria other than the best interests of the organization. Somebody at the top decides, usually on a one-shot basis, which people and departments ought to have the power. The action is akin to allocating monopolies over certain ideas, processes, products, or markets to the "chosen."

The decree isn't made in a vacuum. Positioning and manipulation come to the fore as people vie to be "knighted." The legitimate concept of networking is perverted, so that who you know completely replaces what you know or what you can achieve as a basis for the assignment of power. The assigned power very quickly becomes a status symbol, rather than a tool to be used for a constructive goal. Power is used merely to put one's own personal "stamp" on the surroundings.

Power isn't drained *out* of the organization; it's drained of any useful purpose.

Results of Independence

Independence produces many unhelpful outcomes in organizational life. For instance:

• *Cannibalizing.* One part of the organization can end up devouring the capability or effectiveness of another part. For example, by demanding a lot of attention for their pet projects, some people can use up the best energies of others.

• *Self-centeredness.* Individuals or departments make decisions based solely on how they perceive the results will affect their own power and position. This is true narcissism, where "what's good for me is good for the organization."

• *Aggrandizing.* One person or department takes credit for things done by other people or departments. This is a sort of Darwinian survival of the fittest, where "fittest" is defined as "those who most willing to use available and excessive power to their own advantage."

• *Blaming.* Where personal rights, privilege, turf, and boundaries reign supreme, nothing can be my own (or my department's) fault. With this kind of thinking, independence becomes independence from responsibility.

• *Silence.* One person or department refuses to endorse others' ideas, accomplishments, or value. This is based on the idea that if we support anything other than our own agenda, there will be less money, prestige, influence, or whatever for us.

• *Criticizing.* If we assume that our agenda is the best one, then everyone else must be working on an inferior plan. We use our power to point out these "facts" to the unaware.

• *Insecurity.* We are afraid of what collaboration may cost us. In an independent environment, collaboration appears to reduce our worth and lessen our importance. Sharing information or knowledge could seem like paving the road to being downsized.

• *Hastiness.* To the victor belong the spoils, so we must get there first, regardless of whether we have the best idea or product. Making a splash is more important than filling the tank.

• *Conflict.* Little wars break out everywhere, as tiny nation-states assert their right to be heard. Departmental warfare is the most familiar because it is the oldest and most entrenched. But the age of project and cross-functional teams has brought its own version of the "we're the *real* future of this organization" game.

• *Scarcity.* Since we won't share with each other, resources become stretched and scarce. Helping you means less for me, we believe. The ensuing battles can leave the organization exhausted and impoverished.

• *Contradiction.* So many people, so many ideas, so many projects, all with a different reason for existence—and none related to a common vision (which either doesn't exist or has never been accepted)—lead to inconsistencies, mass confusion, and even blatant contradictions.

• *Waste.* Independent efforts waste organizational resources. If these independents are not working on something that advances the organization's overall position (or at least has the possibility of advancing it), their efforts are wasted even if what they're working on is a reasonable idea.

• *Comparing.* Since pleasure in achieving collaborative goals is absent, the only pleasure that remains is personal victory. But where there are no clear standards of "victory," the only yardstick is to compare ourselves against our enem . . . er, colleagues.

• *Despair.* With all the pieces moving in different directions, nothing of deep and abiding value is created. This produces an organizational despair over the pointlessness of it all.

• *Revenge.* Some of those who have been allowed and encouraged to be independent will start a successful, competing business. Many organizations have created their own competitors, when those energies could have been productively channeled into internal effectiveness.

One other critical point. When we talk about avoiding an independent culture, we're not talking about eliminating radical new initiatives or internal competition to provide services or secure scarce resources. Bold action and internal free markets are crucial elements of the twenty-first-century organization.

But the bold action has to be in pursuit of agreed-upon goals and in collaboration with everyone anywhere (inside or outside the organization) who can make the action as successful as possible. And the internal free markets have to be truly free, free to grow and free to wither, but within agreed-upon boundaries.

We need freedom desperately. But raw independence will leave us dead.

Independent Definitions

Just as in a dependent culture, *initiative* and *collaboration* get redefined in an independent culture.

Initiative means looking out for number one, doing it to them before they do it to you, and finding a way to the top.

Collaboration becomes personal networking, building political alliances, keeping constructive criticism to yourself, and making sure that your name shows up in the right lists of credits.

Initiative gets twisted and true collaboration dies. No incentive exists to get people to work together in any meaningful way. Despite required training in teamwork, communication, sensitivity, and brainstorming, when these people sit down it will still be as a group of independent players only *acting* like a team. If we choose not to dig into the root of our problems, we can end up very frustrated. Why won't these people work together? The answer is that they can't because the structure isn't there, and they won't because the incentive and desire aren't there.

The Death of Independence

Building interdependence is a little like weaving a tapestry; there's a beautiful end result, but the work is meticulous and, at times, tedious. It's easy to stop before it's finished. And one destructively powerful person or group of people can break with the design pattern and destroy the end result. A particularly destructive person can take a pair of power scissors and destroy the tapestry even after it's finished.

Interdependent organizations are long-term projects. They're hard to build and even harder to maintain. There aren't very many of them yet, because they take so long to build and we, as human beings and as a culture, are so damnably focused on the short term. In our shortsightedness, we use our power to get only what we can see today and reap tomorrow.

If that's our view, we can give up on interdependence, and go about our business, which, depending on who we and our people are, will either breed dependence and kill initiative or breed independence and kill collaboration.

And in every organization on the planet today, we need both initiative and collaboration to achieve our dreams and goals.

Notes

1. Paul Johnson, *The Birth of the Modern World Society,* (New York: HarperPerennial, 1992), p. 102.

6

One Side of the Balance: Retaining Power and Exercising Authority

If you wish to know what a man is, place him in authority.

—Yugoslav proverb

She looked out at the sea of faces.

Discouragement. Fear. Distrust. Anger. Belligerence. "Prove it to me." She saw it all as she let her eyes roam around the large room. She felt the grip of panic, and a clear thought ran through her mind: "You made a big mistake when you took this job." She'd only been there for a week and a half, but it felt more like—too long.

Suzanne believed in powersharing. But this bunch? Wasting any power she gave them seemed like the best outcome she could expect from them. Sharing power with the looks she saw on those faces scared her to death. Maybe, this time, command-and-control was the way to go. Put some fire under them. Shake them up. Maybe a few threats.

But Suzanne couldn't do it. She couldn't do it for some crucial reasons. First, she really believed in the efficacy of power-sharing. She had seen it work in many different situations. Second, she had trained herself to be a servant leader—one who was there to clear the way for her team, to make the combined whole work better, not just to make her life easier. Third, she knew there were valid reasons for their anger; their input hadn't been listened to, their recommendations had been generally ignored, and, perhaps worst of all, they hadn't received feedback on anything they had done. Finally, she believed that it was the right thing to do. Running a disempowered and dispirited organization just didn't fit her view of a reasonable way to live her life.

Suzanne resisted the temptation to return to the old hardcase approach just because the organization was in crisis. She wanted to solve the crisis. But she also wanted to lay the groundwork so that there wouldn't be another one close on its heels. "Most crises," her mentor, Jacqueline, had once told her, "are human crises, critical moments that come when people have been undertrained, underutilized, underappreciated, underled, and undertrusted. You don't fix people problems by telling people that they're the problem."

But she also realized that she couldn't fix the people problems by simply "empowering" the people. She knew she would have to go slowly, get them to open up, encourage them to share their concerns, and maybe make some initial suggestions on how they could be corrected. She would have to win some small powersharing victories, and find out who could handle what level of power. In the meantime, she would have to make more decisions than she hoped she would have to make in the long run.

So Suzanne remembered that this was the best way, even if it wasn't the easiest. And then she powershared—carefully.

Legitimate Reasons for Exercising Authority

There are times and situations in which we need to retain power rather than share it. The key questions are when and how do we retain it?

For some people in positions of authority, the answer to the "when" question is "always." A few who take this approach might be able to make a career out of authoritarianism. But for most, it's a ticket to banishment on Elba alongside Napoleon. Even if some things are accomplished, they're done on the backs and broken spirits of dozens, hundreds, or thousands of human "cogs." There's no honor here, probably less accomplishment than could have been achieved with the all-out efforts of many, a lot of wasted intelligence and creativity, and a less-than-enduring legacy.

Unfortunately, it's also hard to leave this attitude behind at the office. Many children live emotionally separated from parents who have chosen to wield absolute authority. Other children, more passive, simply never grow up.

So the best answer to the "when" question is "sometimes." Sometimes—at certain key moments, in certain situations, for certain activities—we as leaders need to retain our power. If the opportunity or challenge is big enough, we may even need to enhance, expand, and extend that power.

But Teddy Roosevelt's "Speak softly and carry a big stick" is not a bad slogan for the exercise of power. Power used constantly deadens itself into a very dull roar. Power is much more effective when it is used sparingly, briefly, even surprisingly. Leaders who exercise authority intelligently 10 percent of the time and who "follow" 90 percent of the time are much more likely to build a dynamic, survivable organization than the 100 percent authoritarians, and are also much more likely to be listened to and followed when they *are* exercising authority.

There are a number of instances in which power should be exercised for the good of others and for the good of the organization:

• *To create (the hard part) and maintain (the other hard part) a lofty, real-world, guiding vision that directs people's thinking and decisions even when we're not standing there.* Knocking down personal, departmental, and divisional barriers to a truly collaborative vision and getting everyone's involvement in and commitment to it are worthy exercises of power. It's *mandatory* that we use our power to get everyone's input to the vision. Even more, we need to ensure that people's ideas—their aspirations—are incorporated in the vision. A vision has to embody people's dreams if we want them to work passionately for it. Nobody gets excited about second-hand dreams.

• *To create much time and space for the leader to do strategic thinking.* That way, the strategic planning of others has both a grid to work from and an anchor to hold it steady. Power used in strategic thinking forces the answer to two questions: What do we do better than anyone else? Does anybody care (that is, does what we "do better" actually add value)?

- *To establish high but achievable expectations, articulated as understandable priorities, that people will agree with and believe they can accomplish.* This is using power to focus on performance and results rather than on behavior and methods (or processes).

- *To put the right people together in the right places at the right times with the right information, knowledge, and resources in order to maximize their chances of success.* Effective leaders act as chemists, mixing ingredients here, separating them there, letting the combinations take on a life and power of their own.

- *To create or permit effective consequences—that is, rewards and recognition for certain results, correction and loss for others.* People should know and feel what the organization needs by having it affect them personally. This is different from the trick-or-treat culture. In the interdependent organization, consequences are agreed-upon results based on the principle of "reaping what you sow." In the trick-or-treat organization, consequences are unilaterally imposed tools of manipulation. The best utilization of power here is to create a broad-brush painting rather than a painting by the numbers. "Today's most effective organizations," in the words of Douglas K. Smith, "operate according to a handful of powerful principles instead of thick manuals of policies and rules."[1]

- *To utilize change—to respond quickly and shrewdly to opportunity, to respond thoughtfully and beneficially to problems, to turn disaster into growth, and to initiate change appropriately.* Most people hate change, but want to work for leaders who use their power to foresee and prepare the organization for it.

- *To instill a culture of passion, creating an organization with "fire in its belly."* We know that without it we will miss the best we can do. Most people, at least in their better moments, want to make a difference. Using power in the form of words, stories, and bold action to tap into that desire and ignite the organization can lead to phenomenal achievement.

• *To make necessary decisions that no other individual, group, or team is able or willing to make.* Only the captain can decide to make a major change of course, and only the captain can decide to abandon ship.

• *To delay or avoid making decisions that are not clearly to the advantage of the organization or that have risks attached (defined or undefined) that may far outweigh the potential benefits.* This means we have to recognize that being decisive clearly includes knowing when *not* to act and then being firm in not acting. "True success is rarely achieved by rushing forward and grabbing the first opportunity that comes along," says psychiatrist and business consultant Martin Groder. "You must be able to wait for critical information to surface so you can make better decisions."[2]

It's the easiest thing in the world to use authority ineffectively, to waste power. Those who exercise legitimate authority spend their power where it counts, on the categories described above, and not on things that others should be able to do with their own power.

And they never, ever, spend it on getting the trappings of power.

Methods of Retaining Power

The answer to the second question, "*How* do we retain and exercise power?" involves a number of key aspects as well:

• *Reserve.* We need to reserve certain decisions (including the decision not to act), or specific components of other decisions, to ourselves.

• *Clarify in writing.* We have to define in simple prose what decisions must be made by us. We have to be very clear about what these kinds of decisions are, for two reasons: first, so others won't usurp our authority; and second, so we will be forced to act when necessary.

• *Seek feedback.* We must determine whether we have retained too much power in given situations. The key question is, "What problems have been caused with any of our stakeholders or goals by the requirement that I make the decision in this situation?"

• *Decide graciously.* We need to let everyone who has a stake in the decision have her "day in court" (whether or not we can do as she suggests). And we need to explain the decision and ensure that we have answered people's concerns, at least to a level where they can support or implement it.

• *Soothe emotions.* Almost all decisions will get an emotional response, although that response can vary widely among people. If we want buy-in to our decisions, we need to recognize and address at least the significant emotional responses.

• *Admit fallibility.* People want to follow leaders who exhibit confidence but who know that they're not God. Few people are as horrible to work for as those who never admit mistakes. We can admit them freely and show how we are correcting them (which will also set a wonderful example).

Power, Rights, and Community

Once we have decided to retain power, we have to apply it in two broad areas that deeply affect the life of the organization: rights and community. We need to balance individual rights and community rights, privacy and the need to know, freedom and justice, the invisible hand of the market and the visible hand of the rule of law. We are in part talking about the dependence-independence continuum. In other words, we have to give people enough power to prevent them from being dependent (which keeps them from becoming all they can be), but not so much as to let them be independent (which keeps the community from becoming all it can be).

We can't really grant people rights. They come with certain of those rights "built in." We either have to believe that or finally give up on the credo that goes like this: "We hold these truths to be self-evident, that all men are created equal; that they are endowed by their Creator with certain unalienable rights. . . ." Indeed, one of the astonishing contradictions about life in a free country is the freedom individuals enjoy as citizens of the nation and the bondage they often experience as employees of the corporation.

Rights come with being human. Status doesn't give us more of them, and lack of status doesn't take them away (although some people will work very hard to do just that).

These rights include freedom of speech, freedom to express opinions in writing, the right to ask questions, access to information, the right to associate (and disassociate), the right to privacy, the right to be treated with dignity and respect, freedom to make and follow through on commitments, and access to justice.[3]

We can use our power to bring these rights to life. We can put power into them. We can build protections around them: We can replace much of our procedure manual with a Magna Carta, a simple and clear statement of the rights we recognize and protect in our organization. This statement needs to focus on power, on what people have the power to do, sentence after sentence that begin: "Our people have the power to. . . ."

As people in authority, we have to use our power to enliven and protect our people's rights. Without those rights, without people knowing that they have them and that they're protected, there is no powersharing. We can tell people until we're blue in the face and they're red in the face that they have power, but if they don't have protected rights, it's just so much blather.

One professional I know was told by his boss that he could make an exception to a restrictive company policy. He operated very successfully for eighteen months with great benefit to the company. But when his action came to the attention of upper management, they took the man apart—while his boss watched silently in fear.

Freedom of Speech

Let's look, as an example of a key right, at freedom of speech. How many organizations really have it? How many people in our organization really believe that they can say what's on their minds and not be criticized, ostracized, or cannibalized for doing so? Without this freedom being *guaranteed in people's minds,* they'll keep their thoughts to themselves, letting us perpetuate bad ideas, valueless activity, inefficient processes, and mistakes, even organizationally fatal mistakes. If people see whistle-blowers and those who speak out with integrity get flogged, we have the death of free speech, an irrecoverable fatality to an organization in any age, and especially in the information age. "The voice of dissent must be heard," warned Henry Ford in his will. And we can't just *say* that we have free speech; we actually have to *guarantee* it. More, we have to protect it. And even more, we have to nurture and encourage it. There are ways of doing this:

- Use anonymous surveys a lot. We should be more afraid of *not* knowing what's on people's minds than we are of knowing it.
- Other than banning character assassination and public ridicule of ideas, assure people that any questions, comments, ideas, inputs, or challenges they have are fair and welcome at meetings.
- Publicly recognize and, when appropriate, reward people who are particularly feisty. "A free society is one where it is safe to be unpopular," statesman Adlai Stevenson reminded us.

What Can't Be Allowed

We also have to apply our power to enliven and protect community. We have to talk in our Magna Carta/Bill of Rights about what *can't* be done, primarily with power, because others have rights. Because we want to use our power to build community and interdependence, we can convert the warnings of Section III of this book into a second part of our Bill of Rights: "Our people do not have the right to use power to. . . ." Make it clear and simple, because otherwise people won't get it or believe it.

To achieve community, power must be applied in the form of control, or nothing will get done. The key question is, "How much control?" To subdue the wild passions of the stallion and turn it into a controlled (but still spirited) being, we have to have some. Without a rule of law, freedom becomes the law of the jungle and survival of the nastiest. We've got to use our power to keep things channeled, without being chained. To take this back to our continuum, we have to have enough control to prevent a destructive independence.

Examples would include using power to require civility in all interactions, to outlaw personal attacks and insults in meetings, to rotate leadership of cross-functional teams among different areas or departments, to require information and knowledge to be shared fluidly, to protect dissent, to relieve oppression, and to eliminate antisocial elements.

A rule of law means a rule of justice. No community can survive or thrive without it. And justice requires a use of power. "Justice without force is powerless," said Blaise Pascal; and then he gave the other side: "Force without justice is tyrannical." And justice implies control. "Order without liberty and liberty without order are equally destructive," warned Theodore Roosevelt.

And therein lies the danger of applying power in the form of control. The rule of law—principles of cooperation and justice—can deteriorate into a list of rules. Rule making is at core a result of hubris: We believe we know more than we do, that we can anticipate all critical events, that we can *control* all critical events. Rule making in a sense is playing God—even though His lists are usually shorter than ours.

With too many rules, freedom dies and is replaced by stagnation and dependence. Playing the game becomes more important than winning it. "That government is best which governs least," advised Thomas Jefferson. We have to use our power to govern, yes. Just not too much.

Limits on Authority

There are always limits on our authority, limits on the manner in which we can exercise power for the good of others. Those limits can come from outside, or they can be imposed from within.

Externally Imposed Limits

It can seem that one of the main missions of the world is to reduce and limit our authority, our ability to use power to achieve our goals. Some of these limits should be resisted, while others should be welcomed.

The limits that should be resisted are the ones that keep us from using power to benefit others. These include:

• *Proposed government rules that we know will not benefit our customers or other stakeholders but are merely being proposed for political reasons.* Often, these rules can actually harm others, by giving people the illusion of benefit or protection or by increasing their costs without giving them a corresponding gain.

• *Work rules or industry practices that have the ostensible purpose of "saving jobs," but in reality make our organization less competitive and less likely to survive.* For example, rigid divisions of work, which permit only certain predesignated people to perform certain activities, are destined to make us uncompetitive.

• *Jealous and envious attacks from others.* Human beings throughout history have seldom been enamored of authority; in a democratic and relatively free society, they can positively loathe it. If we want to invite attacks, assaults, slander, and opposition, the simplest way is to attempt to exercise authority. People who have nothing positive to contribute will relish the opportunity to tear us down. If we're not careful, we can begin limiting our use of authority in order to avoid the confrontations.

The limits that should be welcomed are those that in themselves benefit others, including our stakeholders. Among these are:

• *Standard industry practices.* For example, commonality of design and interchangeableness of components as desired by our customers and accepted by our competitors.

• *Reasonable governmental enforcement of environmental practices that individuals by themselves or the workings of the market alone cannot ensure.* For example, if we're the only ones pouring effluent into the river, it might not be a problem; if we all do it, the river dies.

• *Ethical standards that allow our stakeholders to trust our products or services and raise our work above the level of* caveat emptor *("let the buyer beware").* Professional politicians and car dealers have a reputation for disregarding these limits; doctors, architects, and engineers are generally expected to uphold professional standards of excellence.

• *The demands of a knowledge-based economy.* "It is impossible to have effective knowledge exchange in a command and control structure,"[4] writes Hubert Saing-Onge. Knowledge is simply too vast, too changeable, and too esoteric to be understood and transferred up and down the layers of a pyramid. In effect, we can have the illusion of control or we can have the reality of collective and expanding knowledge. The voluntary limit on our power to "control" knowledge can lead to limitless possibilities.

Internally Imposed Limits

Just as a mystery can be more intriguing than an exposé and partial disrobing can be more seductive than pornography, so power cloaked can be more effective than naked power. As the old saying has it, "If you want everyone to listen, just whisper."

Authority that wants to be heard learns how to whisper. It puts voluntary restraints on itself. It doesn't do this just so there will be some power left over to share with others. It does this because it wants to be powerful, to have the most effect for good that it can possibly have, to really be *heard*.

One of the astonishing voluntary practices of the first 150 years of U.S. history (1788–1940) was that no president served more than two terms even though no external limit proscribed the practice. Their view was that public service wasn't a profession; it was, instead, a piece of an engaged, active, and otherwise useful life. We sometimes see this principle followed by retiring

CEOs and older employees who yield power and then mentor those to whom they have yielded it. (We would do well to apply this principle elsewhere in our organizations—for example, by making staff work a piece of a career path that includes before and after stints in line/operating positions.)

This practice of laying down power was so revolutionary in the history of the world and so appreciated by the American people that a short time after one man violated it (Franklin Roosevelt, twice) an externally imposed limit (a constitutional amendment) was put in place to guarantee it. Since few in Congress "get it" and understand the importance of voluntary restraints on power, it seems almost inevitable that they, too, will eventually be forced to accept externally imposed term limits.

It isn't always beneficial to do everything that we can do. We've paid for the buffet and have the right to go through the line one more time, but the greater act may be the choice to pass. We're paying the bills and have the right to decide where we go on vacation, but the greater act may be the choice to go where the others involved desire. We have the position and the right to do or decide a hundred things, but the greater act may be the choice to leave ninety of these things to others.

To be an effective authority, we can't always use all the power that we have at our disposal. Our tendency may well be the opposite: "What's the use of having it if I don't use it?" But like the interest in a savings account, the return on unspent power (that is, influence) grows faster when we *don't* use it, when we leave a portion of what we've earned untapped.

This means that we let someone we're grooming lead a negotiation that we could ace. We let others in a meeting express their positions and ask the questions while we simply listen. We could decide to do something one way but then defer to a team consensus to do it differently. And all the while, our authority is legitimized and our influence grows.

In a sense, power is transactional so we can't "save it up." But while the power to take a specific action at that moment might be lost, the gain in total influence, in total aura of power to the person in authority can be substantial. In essence, we're saving up the energy from the power *not* transacted in a different form to be used on the "biggies" when they come.

We should be especially careful to limit ourselves when we get the "do goods": "I'm only going to use this power for this good cause." We've got to beware the "do good" feeling, because we're all a little too imperfect and driven by complex motives (and perhaps by dysfunction or self-deception) to allow ourselves to be swept off our feet by those "save the organization" or "save the world" ideas. Many of the fads and the excellent ideas (including open-book management, total quality management, business process reengineering) that have been applied to the wrong situations have been implemented because somebody in authority combined his unrestrained power with a "do good" idea that didn't apply to the actual illness of the organization. We should use power to do good, but not to be a do-gooder.

Unless leaders are willing to rely totally on brute force (which is a surprisingly fragile form of power, as Louis XVI and Marie Antoinette discovered), their power is also limited by the expectations and convictions of their followers. That is to say, effective leaders have to lead, to a certain extent, by *following*. We have to take the pulse of our followers, to see where they and our culture at large are going. Then we have to mold our leadership style to take advantage of this knowledge. What British prime minister Benjamin Disraeli said (with a touch of irony) has truth in organizational life: "I must follow the people. Am I not their leader?"

Another way of saying this is that followers will follow with different levels of enthusiasm and commitment depending on how well we as leaders follow their lead. If we lead by fear and run roughshod over their thoughts, feelings, needs, and goals, we will get grudging support and substantial undercutting. If, on the other hand, we connect our thoughts, feelings, needs, and goals to theirs, they will follow passionately because they're actually following themselves. They are following their own ideas which have now been embodied in us as their leaders.

This means, however, that we have to do more than merely discover majority thinking or the consensus of the group and then shape it into a mission statement. Politicians have become experts at taking polls and turning the results into action plans (which is a perverse sort of leading by following, akin to following a car by sticking our heads up the exhaust pipe). Instead, we have to form our group's desires into something new. We have to pick out the malignant parts and lose them. And we have to take the majestic parts, the parts that have intrinsic value, and tie them intimately to the needs of our customers and the vision of our organization.

Limits aren't bad. Limits, in fact, keep things "good." Uncontrolled power—power without limits—all too easily separates from its lofty goals and degenerates into "salvation" by imposition.

Overcoming the Obstacles to Effective Exercise of Authority

Some of us have so thoroughly grasped the concept that limits on power keep it ethical, useful, and vigorous—in short, good— that we've moved to the other extreme: We share power when we shouldn't. Why, at times, do we fail to exercise authority when it is needed? There are three major reasons:

1. *Confusion.* When we don't know what to do, passing the problem along to someone else can be very appealing. "Maybe somebody will be able to help me out on this." But delegating confusion is unlikely to produce clarity. Powersharing works only in the context of clearly defined and widely understood visions, priorities, expectations, and goals. We can also be confused about how much authority we should exercise if we don't see that the answer can vary from organization to organization and within an organization over time.

2. *Laziness.* This is where powersharing becomes a way not to have to do things ourselves. In reality, powersharing with others doesn't make the leader's job go away; in fact, it may make the job of leading both more necessary and more difficult. When people are disempowered and little is happening, leadership can become little more than putting the organization on cruise control. When a lot of people begin to exercise power, then creativity, new directions, internally initiated changes, ambiguity, and

even chaos can fill the organization with much new energy and many new possibilities needing to be led.

3. *Desire to Be "Liked."* If being "liked" (which we can get from people by telling them what they want to hear or giving them what they want) is a high personal priority, we can end up powersharing when retention is the best answer. "I don't want to appear heavy-handed," "I want everyone to be involved." These phrases sound very good, but there are times when everyone should not be involved and when our hand, no matter how heavy it seems, must be the one that is raised.

The result of sharing power when we should be retaining it is that everyone can take initiative in counterproductive ways. There is an excess of power beyond what is needed or can intelligently and wisely be handled, and the excess usually goes into independent mischief. "So what is the conflict? Well, in order to empower your people, you must not interfere with their work. Alas, sometimes, in order to make sure that the job gets done, you don't have any choice but to interfere," writes Eliyahu M. Goldratt.[5]

Leaders must be willing to retain power and exercise authority whenever the situation warrants it. And only when the situation warrants it.

Notes

1. Douglas K. Smith, "The Following Part of Leading," in Frances Hesselbein, Marshall Goldsmith, and Richard Beckhard, eds., *The Leader of the Future* (San Francisco: Jossey-Bass, 1996), p. 202.
2. Martin Groder, "The Power of Strategic Waiting," *Bottom Line Personal*, 1 October, 1997, p. 17.
3. For an excellent treatment of this issue of rights, see Gifford and Elizabeth Pinchot, *The Intelligent Organization* (San Francisco: Berrett-Koehler Publishers, 1996), especially chapter 5.
4. Hubert Saing-Onge, "Tacit Knowledge: The Key to the Strategic Alignment of Intellectual Capital," *Strategic Leadership*, April 1996, p. 14.
5. Eliyahu M. Goldratt, "A TOC Approach to Organizational Empowerment," *APICS*, April 1997, p. 45.

7

The Other Side of the Balance: Sharing Power and Yielding Authority

Management's ability to get the best from people increases when it chooses to share its power.

—Tony Kizilos and Roger P. Heinisch, *Harvard Business Review*, September/October 1986

Powersharing releases.

Powersharing is releasing the creative and productive capabilities of our people by two actions. First, we have to provide "stuff": clear goals, necessary training, required resources, appropriate incentives, and the freedom to select means and methods. And second, we have to remove barriers: internal and external obstacles to the achievement of agreed-upon goals.

Powersharing is not simply making a declaration that "our people have power." The declaration is fine, but it's not enough. Abraham Lincoln considered the Emancipation Proclamation, which freed the slaves, his highest achievement, but it had no effect until some very strong actions were taken on the battlefield.

Powersharing means nothing unless our people have what *we* have: the ability to act in a powerful way. They must have whatever is necessary to enable them to make decisions and have them stick, to take a new direction and not be pulled over and given a ticket.

And they have to have the inevitable roadblocks removed. Some of those roadblocks are internal—their own fears, insecurities, and ignorance, to name a few. And some are external—bureaucratic systems, counterproductive policies, archaic procedures, and political "power centers." The people themselves, with our help and support, will have to take steps to remove some of these obstacles. Others, only we will be able to demolish.

Powersharing is in part a process of sharing our power, and in part a decision to use our power in a more expansive, abundant, and generous way. True powersharing is creative: It creates new opportunities for power to be exercised; it releases power that has previously been blocked. And it is multiplicative: It increases our overall power and the reach of that power. What seems at first blush to be a paradox is really a stunning reality: Yielding power can lead to more organizational power and at the same time enhance our own.

But powersharing is no panacea. It won't solve or even address all our problems. And it will create new problems of its own. This is in part why almost everyone talks about "empowerment" but most do so very little true powersharing.

The Importance of Powersharing

Most of the revolutions in history have been triggered by disempowerment. When people finally feel that they have no power, that they have, in fact, nothing to lose, they can become very liberated in their actions and very dangerous to the continued life of the nation—or corporation.

One of the unavoidable, captivating impressions we'll acquire if we talk to people at middle and lower levels in modern organizations is a pervasive sense of disempowerment. You can see it in their eyes, hear it in their flat tones, perceive it in their questions. Hundreds of people at seminars I have given—people from small organizations and Fortune 500 corporations, from family-owned businesses to multinational conglomerates—have let me see into their organizations.

What I see is too much disempowerment.

Speeches won't make it go away. Good intentions won't change the frustrations. Even promises won't cure this malaise. In fact, unkept promises will actually make it worse. The only thing that changes this reality is the willingness to face it and its effects and to begin working for a balance of power.

It's too easy to be frustrated with our lack of necessary power on the way up and then to forget that feeling once we get there. We hated the powerlessness, and maybe hated the bosses who wouldn't share the power. Then we acquire power and can too easily become like those we hated.

And become hated ourselves.

Areas in Which to Powershare

We can share power in a number of ways:

• *By providing information.* Although information isn't power, it's a doorway into power. Give it away. Watch it multiply. Hidden and hoarded information, not power, corrupts. All of us have some level of need to be allowed in, to be "in the know," to be on the inside. The very act of sharing information is powerful, drawing an intellectual and emotional response from the listener and triggering new combinations and possibilities. When information isn't shared, people still have the same need to know; but now, the blanks are filled in with gossip, scuttlebutt, trial balloons, hidden agendas, and manipulation. "The hoarding of power and information," claims Oren Harari, "is a sign of an insecure, ineffectual manager, not a strong one."[1]

• *By sharing responsibility.* Few people are really challenged to do what they're capable of, and even fewer actually get stretched. We're not talking about work load here. Many of us are overloaded. But mostly it's with things that aren't difficult for us to do, and way too often it's with things that don't need to be done. Unload people, take away the junk, use power to prevent the wasting of their time and lives. And then fill them up with work that matters.

• *By giving authority.* People need the legitimate power to make decisions without clearing everything first with someone higher up. In fact, if people have to clear most things, they are inherently *not* decision makers. Impress on people the broad range of decision-making capability they have. When in doubt, tell them to make the decision—or get help from other people so they can make it well. Tell them to let people who are interdependently connected to the decision know about it, and make sure they know that this might *not* include you.

• *By encouraging spending.* People who can't spend money have no power. Period. Money is the language of a free economy. People who can't spend it have no language, have no voice. The organization has cut out their tongues. Give people parameters, to be sure, but make them as big as possible, not as limited as possible. Get upset when people *don't* ever spend money. Somewhere beyond prudence lies impotence.

• *By providing resources.* How can people have power if they have no tools? Give people a range of resources. Encourage them to *imagine* what they need to excel, whether or not you even have it available, even if their requests are unreasonable.

• *By granting access.* Interdependence demands access to people outside as well as inside the organization. Get rid of the barriers. Be unwilling ever to hear the comment, "I didn't know I could just call the supplier" (or customer, or affiliate in Thailand). In medieval society, people couldn't rise above their class or initiate conversation with whomever they chose. Often, their station in life was highlighted by the very clothes they were permitted to wear. Their manner of dress defined them. Today, it's the organization chart and the policy and procedure manual. At least the clothing idea isn't boring.

• *By ensuring time for thinking.* An idea that seems to be missing from our downsized, rightsized, delayered, fast-paced world is that people actually need time to *think*. Just as we should use our power to create the time and space that we need for thinking, we should powershare with our people so that they too can have the time needed to think. Mindless action and being "busy" are miserable substitutes for thought, creativity, and innovation. The message in too many organizations is, "We'd better not catch you thinking. Do it on your own time. Can't you see we've got *work* to do?" There is little or no power in going through the motions, even if we do it really fast. Power germinates and grows in the seedbed of time.

• *By taking an interest.* No one really has usable power if she loathes what she does. Weed the false advertising out of résumés and interviews. Work hard to know who your people are. And work just as hard to assign them to positions that they are interested in and value, and put them on teams where their best thinking will be stimulated and appreciated.

• *By giving reasons.* We powershare with people when we tell them the "whys" of what we're asking them to do. Tell people the reasons that an assignment is important. Tell them why you chose *them* to do it, which, if handled well, can be a dignifying as well as powersharing action.

• *By extending emotional support.* Last but not least, and maybe often most, is powersharing by giving needed emotional support. This support truly draws out power, whether it comes in the form of recognition, appreciation, gratitude, personal sympathy, empathy, mentoring, helping out in a crisis, forgiveness, or just listening. A dispirited organization is by definition disempowered, but we can do something about it. The day of the "rational only" approach to leadership is gone. It needed to be.

Requirements for Powersharing

Surely we need powerful people who know how to use their power. They need to learn, largely through a process of trial and growth (trial and "error" is an inherently disempowering statement or process), when to do and when to ask, when to show initiative and when to be restrained. They, like us, need to know when to use their power and when to share it.

To help them use their power effectively, there are a number of crucial foundational requirements that must be in place:

• *A truth-speaking atmosphere.* If people can't or won't speak the truth for whatever reason, powersharing becomes a bad joke. Speaking the truth includes "thinking out loud" about questions or concerns, admitting mistakes or ignorance, and thinking and talking about ideas that aren't part of the "accepted norm" within the culture. "When a leader creates an atmosphere in which employees feel free to offer contrary views and speak the truth, an empowered work force is created."[2] Speaking the truth, of course, doesn't include belittlement of others.

• *A free environment.* "Let us not be unmindful that liberty is power," said John Quincy Adams to Congress in 1825.[3] The psychological and historical reality is that free minds work better than those in bondage do. Restrictions on liberty by their very nature will put boundaries around a person's dreams, thoughts, and creativity. An experienced consultant who cares about the difference can tell within a very short period of time if a culture is breathing liberty or not.

• *Available options.* To say that people have power when they have few or no choices is a contradiction in terms. While liberty means a right to choose, having choices is what gives liberty its practical value. The exercise of power presupposes having an array of choices. To have only one choice is to be weak. And to have options that we don't know exist or don't understand is to be weak. We need to create the options, as many as necessary to make our people strong, and then help them to become comfortable with making choices. As said earlier, genuine options must include the authority to spend money. Employees who have to go through a maze of approvals to get office supplies do *not* have power. Choices inherently make people powerful. And service without choice equals slavery.

• *A failure-friendly culture.* A big part of powersharing is granting people the freedom to make mistakes, to try and fail without them having to deny it in order to protect themselves and without us blaming and shaming them. When we can celebrate failure, including rewarding people for spectacular mistakes (that is, mistakes that come from actions which had tremendous potential, which taught us much, and which didn't put the organization itself at risk), we've created something so freeing, so unusual, and so uplifting, that people will blossom around us.

• *Training.* People are going to need skills that they never had need of before. People won't just "pick up" how to handle power and how to work interdependently with others who are also exercising new-found power. We'll have to train them in how to communicate, collaborate, negotiate, plan, follow up, and solve problems. This can happen, but it won't just happen without effort. They'll also need to be shown what the prevailing policies, procedures, and guidelines are, how to operate successfully within the organizational culture, and how to interpret and meet organizational expectations. We almost can't do too much training.

• *A new support structure.* The old structure of monitoring, directing, and controlling has to give way to a new structure that will ensure results. Putting *self* in front of each of those words would point us in the right direction. This means effectively using performance agreements,[4] forward-looking performance evaluations,[5] performance improvement plans,[6] self-selected training (possibly including "declaring a major"—an area of chosen expertise that the organization can use), accountability with self-measurement and reporting, and built-in consequences (positive and negative). Surely these consequences should be tied in with the quantity of future power held. For example, success at one level could ensure access to bigger and more important projects and greater levels of organizational resources. We should structure our powersharing in such a way that more power is shared or drawn out where it is already being constructively used.

• *Long-term commitment.* We can't "try out" powersharing to see it if "works." Our lack of real confidence in powersharing as an abiding philosophy will be conveyed to everyone, whether we articulate it in words or not. We have to be willing to stick with it no matter what, and especially through the early stages when people are first exercising their new-found power and screwing things up.

• *Accountability.* When we powershare with people, they must be made to understand that a day of reckoning will come when they will be held accountable for how they used that power. The management maxim says that "what gets measured gets done," which may not always be true. But it's fairly certain that if it doesn't get measured, it won't get done. Two key items *must* be included in performance evaluations:

1. Log of major mistakes, how they were corrected, and what was learned. People, if they're doing anything with their power, will make mistakes. The shorter this list, the worse it is.
2. Log of innovations, including their impact (for example, value to the customer, cost reduction, process improvement).

These logs should be controlled and filled out by each person, not by us. Powersharing assumes that people old enough to work are old enough to track their own performance.

Methods of Powersharing

There are certain steps we can take to make powersharing work:

1. *Powershare slowly.* Don't rush it. We're in it for the long haul. We'll inevitably have to do some regrouping and rethinking along the way.

2. *Start small.* Give people the power to achieve some fairly sure, bite-sized goals so that they can "try it out" and feel successful at it. Don't overwhelm people by going straight from hierarchy to self-directed teams.

3. *Educate continually.* Powersharing means that people are going to have to do some things for the first time. Two of the most difficult and anxiety-producing are making choices (such as selecting resources) and making decisions (for instance, choosing a plan and implementing it). Nobody knows how to do these things, or has the confidence to try, without some training and practice.

4. *Create expectations.* People will be driven to use their newly acquired power if they have some targets to hit that are beyond what they can do with lower levels of power.

5. *Create opposition.* Whether it's "they don't think we can do it" or a challenging deadline, opposition energizes people and causes them to use any power at their disposal to surmount it.

6. *Use silence.* Don't solve their problems for them. Don't give them the answer. Don't say anything at the meeting, including using telltale body language. Listening without talking or solving or deciding is an essential powersharing tool, if for no other reason than the fact that people can't stand silence and will counter it with talk.

7. *Instill optimism.* We must continually let people know that we believe in them, in what they can do with their power, in their ability to reach their objectives.

8. *Remove obstacles.* If we ask our people what's disempowering them, whether these obstacles are internal to them or external to the organization, they'll tell us, so long as we've created a truth-telling atmosphere. Although they will have to remove many of these obstacles themselves (perhaps with some encouragement and training), we will have to remove some of them. One of the most important things a leader can do is to eliminate people's excuses for not performing.

9. *Evaluate carefully.* "The tongue has the power of life and death," the old proverb reminds us. Comments made too soon (such as "I'm not sure this powersharing stuff is working") are almost guaranteed to be a self-fulfilling prophecy. We have to evaluate, to see if we need to do anything differently, but we can't let the evaluation itself become a determining factor in our powersharing. On the other hand, our carefully chosen and timed words can bring about needed correction when the power is being wasted or misused.

10. *Reallocate continuously.* Power must be reevaluated and reallocated constantly. Very quickly, we can end up with an excess here (producing independence) or a shortfall there (producing dependence). "As [birds] fly in formation it's clear that

there must be a leader," writes Wolfgang E. Grulke, "but the leader changes with the wind—first one bird, then another. In the same way . . . the leader [in the business] is the one that happens to make the most sense at the time."[7]

Effective leaders don't look at reevaluating power as a chore but rather as one of their most important functions. It's much easier to assign power on a one-time basis to a fixed location, such as a department, but we'll pay for that ease with all the costs of an imbalance of power.

Power ought to be less associated with positions and more associated with results. Here a person leads a team, there she is part of a team; here she makes the decision alone, there she merely advises. It means putting power where it can add value, not prestige. It's power as a tide rather than a holding tank. In any reorganization or reengineering, one of the key questions— almost never asked or answered—is how will (or should) power be reallocated? Answering this question well can open the door to great opportunities. Answering it badly, or not at all, can lead to disaster.

"How can you spot a powerful person? Look at his or her results. Are these people directly or indirectly responsible for getting a lot done? And especially, are they somehow responsible for getting a lot done through others?"[8]

False Powersharing

"My job description is a joke," Desirée moaned as she scanned the six-page document.

Kara stuck her head inside the door. "More to do than time to do it?" she asked.

Desirée shoved the document away and slumped in her chair. "Come on in and sit down," she said, motioning to a chair next to her desk. "The problem isn't what the job description says. It's what it doesn't *say. It covers about a third of my responsibilities, a fourth of my duties, and just about zero of my expected results."*

"Welcome to the club."

"I don't get it. They go to all this trouble to write these

elaborate job descriptions, which don't mean a blasted thing. They're incomplete from the get-go. Then they downsize, and you get more work, but no more authority. You do a good job, and you get more work as a 'reward.' And they never take anything away.

Kara nodded. "Don't forget invisible downsizing."

"What do you mean?"

"Well, I've got the same number of people in my department as two years ago, so it looks like we haven't been downsized. But our work load is up about 40 percent. That, to me, is 'invisible downsizing.' Invisible, but very real."

"The thing that beats all," Desirée sighed, "is that they don't call it 'downsizing' for the survivors. They christen it 'empowerment.' "

We have to be careful not to play the "dump/blame" game or allow others to do it to us.

It is possible to abdicate responsibility—but not give up our power—under the guise of powersharing. We give them the responsibility without the authority, the load without the shovel. Then we blame them for their failure, which is really our failure.

We can call this a failure of "empowerment," when it's really a failure of *dis*empowerment. The formula is this: More responsibility + no change in power = disempowerment. People so encumbered will actually be *less* capable of doing what they need to do.

We must not let powersharing become dumping in disguise or a cover-up for ruthless downsizing that buries those left behind.

Overcoming the Reasons We Don't Powershare

Even if we see the value of powersharing, there can be some internal drivers that keep us from doing it.

These drivers include:

• *Fear.* It's easy, in the course of a career, to begin worrying about being knocked off our perch and to become hypervigilant about real and perceived threats to our authority. It took a lot of effort—and perhaps fighting and clawing—to get to where we are, and we sense that it wouldn't take much to drop us off the radar screen. This fear is compounded by the facts that we've all been let down and betrayed, and there really are some rotten people out there. Fear is a paralyzing monster, and we may respond by trying to control and do everything ourselves—to our own and the organization's detriment. To deal effectively with fear, we must do two things: first, realize that there *is* danger out there and take steps to minimize its negative impact; and second, give ourselves permission to be human, to be afraid without letting that fear paralyze us.

• *Lack of trust.* While fear relates more to our own internal insecurities, lack of trust relates more to the reality of what people really are. Most of us have a hard time trusting people, *really* trusting people. And the rest of us who do easily trust people probably shouldn't be that way. The fact is, we shouldn't trust people because they're trustworthy (they often aren't), but rather because it's the right thing to do and leads to the greatest overall success for ourselves and our organizations. Naïveté will get us killed, because we won't be prepared for the inevitable letdowns. We have to expect that some people are going to betray our trust and waste our attempts at powersharing. We can minimize the risks by following the steps in this book and by not trusting some people at all, but sometimes we'll guess wrong and sometimes people will change in a negative direction. If we're planning to powershare only when humanity becomes trustworthy, we've got a really long wait on our hands.

• *Desire to control.* People with power can be led, but they're very hard to control. The problem is that even a tyrannical, completely disempowered organization has only the *illusion* of control. We can't make people admit mistakes, openly tackle and correct problems, make suggestions, and take initiative in a controlled environment. The fear of committing—of doing something wrong—simply outweighs the fear of omitting—of not doing something beneficial. And we have no control over the external environment. When the tsunami is heading for our ship and we can't see it because we're in our cabin planning new disciplinary procedures, none of our people on deck will warn us, and our tightly controlled, orderly, precise little operation will come to rest peacefully on the bottom of the sea.

• *Impatience.* We want to see immediate results from our "powersharing initiative." If we don't, we might be tempted to take all the power back into our own hands. But powersharing isn't an "initiative," it's a way of life. People who are only looking at the next month or quarter or who don't plan to stay around very long don't have the attitude necessary to make powersharing work. "Someone who is patient is greater than a warrior," the proverb tells us. In fact, it's a lot easier to fight than it is to wait. We can expect to see results, but we should expect them to be uneven—more from this person or team than that, some false starts here and an occasional flash of brilliance over there.

• *Ignorance.* If we don't know who our people really are (their personalities, interests, values, and capabilities), we will be very reluctant to powershare with them. The most effective leaders get past this ignorance, whatever its cause (for example, it's harder to analyze people than processes, people wear masks, it takes a lot of time). Ineffective leaders think of their people simplistically, often as stereotypes or caricatures.

The result of not powersharing is that nobody else takes initiative, except the initiative to take the temperature of those in formal authority and to avoid making a "CLM" (career-limiting move). The chances of our organizations succeeding over time if we're the only ones taking initiative are much lower than the chances of our organizations shriveling up and withering away.

Giving power away will require us to overcome some personal challenges, but it's worth the effort for us as well as for our people. "Willingness to surrender power is not a character flaw; it's a sign of good health."[9]

Here's to your organization's health.

The Power of Powersharing

Powersharing doesn't mean moving people into *positions* of power but rather letting people have power over their work and lives. This means that everyone can exercise personal power without moving into a formal leadership role.

An astonishing number of people with personalities and temperaments unsuited to permanent positions of leadership are put into those positions. Often, it's because they are good at actually doing the work or simply because they don't cause any trouble. It may be that we subtly, and falsely, conclude that to powershare with them means to promote them. If they're unsuited to the role, however, they are actually disempowered by promotion.

The military has seen in crisis after crisis that officers made and promoted in peacetime are often unsuited to be wartime leaders. In many cases, organizations are promoting peacetime performers, such as steady workers and analysts, into "officer" roles, forgetting the reality that the peaceful marketplace of a generation ago has given way to the battle-torn, take-no-prisoners marketplace. World War III is already a reality, but it's an economic rather than a military war. "Promotion should not be more important than accomplishment, or avoiding instability more important than taking the right risk," advises Peter Drucker.

We have to powershare with people where they are. Although few may be qualified to be positional leaders, nearly everyone can lead something—their own effort, a selected project, a certain team. Flexible powersharing with an interdependent work-force is the crucial form our efforts have to take.

True powersharing is more akin to unleashing a racehorse than to plugging someone in to a power source. The power is already there, inside the person, waiting to be unwrapped. The great leaders of every age and every sphere of life have learned how to do this, and have done it well.

So can we.

Notes

1. Oren Harari, "Leadership vs. Autocracy: They Just Don't Get It!" *Management Review*, August 1996, p. 44.

2. Warren Bennis and Robert Townsend, *Reinventing Leadership* (New York: William Morrow, 1995), p. 73.
3. As quoted in Paul Johnson, *The Birth of the Modern* (New York: HarperPerennial, 1992), p. 61.
4. See Stephen Covey's works, especially *Principle-Centered Leadership* (New York: Simon & Schuster, 1991), Chapter 18.
5. See Dick Grote, *The Complete Guide to Performance Appraisal* (New York: AMACOM, 1996).
6. See V. Clayton Sherman, *From Losers to Winners* (New York: AMACOM, 1987).
7. Wolfgang E. Grulke, "The New Workplace: The Changing Nature of Work, Organizations and Business in the Information Economy," *AFSM International,* September 1997, p. 31.
8. Robert L. Dilenschneider, *On Power* (New York: HarperCollins, 1994), p. 11.
9. Dr. Robert Hemfelt, Dr. Frank Minirth, and Dr. Paul Meier, *Love Is a Choice* (Nashville: Thomas Nelson Publishers, 1989), p. 136.

8

Finding the Quantity Balance Through Interdependence

Nothing destroyeth authority so much, as the unequal and untimely interchange of power pressed too far, and relaxed too much.

—Sir Francis Bacon, *Essays: Of Empire*, 1597

Meg smiled at John.

"You did an absolutely outstanding job on the scheduling system project," she said warmly. "I knew when I gave you that assignment that there were a lot of loose ends, things that I couldn't tell you about because I didn't know about them. But you managed to pull it all together and fill in the blanks."

"I had a good group of people to work with," John said, nodding. "I have to admit, I was a little scared when I agreed to take it on. I knew I didn't know enough to pull it off."

Meg paused for a moment. "That was one of the main reasons behind my asking you to do it. I knew you were scared, and I knew you didn't know enough."

John looked surprised, almost astonished. "I . . . I don't understand."

Meg leaned back. "John, every time in my career when I've assigned an 'expert' to a project like this, all I get back are the 'expert' solutions. They're too steeped in the 'best ways' of doing things to look at it with new eyes. They 'know' a lot of stuff that isn't even true anymore, if it ever was. And another big problem with them is that they aren't scared."

John was puzzled. "You want *people to be scared?"*

"I do," Meg said, nodding. "I don't want people to be afraid, but I want them to be scared." Noting the look on his face, she leaned forward. "John, when people aren't a little scared—a little unsure of themselves, a little uncertain about their ability to pull it off, a little overwhelmed by the assignment and the mystery of it—it scares the hell out of me. I don't want people to be afraid about making mistakes and being treated unjustly, but I really do want them to be scared about the unknowns and grays of a major assignment."

"I think I see where you're heading," John nodded. "Being scared makes you do your homework. It makes you think about things from a whole new perspective or angle. And . . ."

"And?"

"And it makes you look around for help."

"Exactly. You know that you might not even know enough to ask the right questions yet. You do a lot of looking and listening. And then asking. Asking for ideas. Asking where your thinking is off base. And asking people to bring their interest and skills—along with their questions and confusion—into the battle with you."

John set his notebook down on the front of the desk and sat back in his chair. "I had to do all those things. I even invited two people to help me who had no background in scheduling systems, so they could help us think 'out of the box.'"

"John," Meg said slowly. "You are valuable in part because you know what you don't know and are willing to admit it. That opens the way for you to bring all kinds of talent to bear on a problem or opportunity. You know you can't go it alone, but you don't dump things on people. You've got balance. You get the best out of your people, but you still make the decisions when you need to."

"Thanks. I'll try to live up to that."

"Well," Meg smiled, "you're going to get a chance in a hurry. Our biggest supplier has just had a big reorganization. Some of the people we've worked with for years have been

*moved elsewhere or are just gone. We've got to get in there fast
and sort out this relationship. I want you to do it. Are you
ready?"*

*"But I don't . . ." John reached for his notebook, opened it,
and took out his pen. He wrote a few sentences, and then looked
back at Meg. "Ready," he said firmly, with a smile.*

A Critical Change in Attitude

A long, detailed, and at times ferocious debate has raged in the
organizational literature for many years now: Are leaders and
managers different? Do leaders also have to manage? Do the best
managers take on the persona of a leader? Is one better than the
other? What, exactly, *is* a leader or a manager?

The answer to these questions, from a different direction, is
this: Everybody in a position or role of authority is a leader.
Everyone who is leading anyone or anything is a leader. These
people might be good leaders or bad leaders, they might lead
people up the mountain or straight to hell, they might lead by
getting out in front and pulling or by circling to the rear and
pushing (or kicking), but *they're all leaders. Not* managers.

The reason? As discussed in Chapter 2, we can't really "manage" anything or anyone other than ourselves. We can try. We
can use prodigious energy and effort, miles of red tape, rules
and restrictions, fear and sticks to attempt to control the efforts
of others. It works, to a limited extent, if we want to run a machine whose moving (and lifeless) parts happen to be human
beings. Henry Ford showed us the way. It works if we're trying
to control something where every breath can be monitored and
measured and critiqued and adjusted. But God help us if we
need creativity, or suggestions, or hearts and minds instead of
just bodies.

Leaders who illude that they are managers of others can be
dangerous to the health and life of the organization. A lot of what
these managers call "management," warns organizational savant
Peter Drucker, becomes the process of making it hard for people
to do their jobs. Caela Farren and Beverly L. Kaye caution, "[An]
important trend is *an erosion of confidence* . . . in the manage-

ment caste, which occupies structural positions that require leadership, but does not provide it."[1] Managers themselves can become frustrated at the impossibility of managing the unmanageable, at trying to control implacably willful and resistant human beings.

The reality is that everyone who is "in charge" has to be a leader, while allowing—no, *insisting*—that everyone under his authority become a self-manager. Life is too short to baby-sit grown people. Once we see this truth clearly—that everyone with authority is by definition a leader, and everyone else by definition is a self-manager—everything else begins to fall into place in a new way.

Leaders release and managers constrict. Perfect. Somebody has to release the power and energy and movement, and that's us if we're in authority. But we just can't have this stuff flying all over the place. Somebody has to control it, constrict it, give it a detailed shape and form. Who is that? It's the manager. Who's the manager? The person doing the work.

Leaders have a goal of creating an innovative environment that will of necessity produce mistakes, and managers have a goal of honing their craft to reduce and eliminate mistakes and waste. Two different jobs, both of them necessary. We in authority—leaders—need to welcome and even celebrate mistakes, while those doing the work—managers—need to focus on learning from and never repeating those mistakes.

Leaders focus on the big picture and results, while managers focus on the job at hand and methods. Both jobs are crucial. Somebody has to know where this ship is going and what the destination will look like when we get there. That's the leader, the person with authority. But somebody else had *better* focus on the job of navigation and on making sure that the system works, or we won't reach our destination. That's the self-manager. There's no conflict here. Just a clear differentiation of responsibility.

Leaders use trust and managers use self-control. Given what we've already discussed, you can see the complementary nature of these tools. It's not an either-or, one-is-better-than-the-other kind of proposition. If we're in authority, we design an organizational environment, a social architecture, that oozes trust. What

kind of trust? *That people—managers—will control themselves.*
Somebody has to trust. That's the leader. And somebody else—
the self-manager, of course—has to control.

Leaders do have some managerial responsibility. What is
that? To do the details of their own job in a self-managed, self-
controlled way. And managers do have some leadership responsibility. And that is? To lead by example, to do their work in a
way that only an excellent manager could deliver, and to lead as
the need arises.

We with authority are leaders. We've got to start thinking of
ourselves that way. (Whether we're good at it is another question
altogether.) And we've got to stop acting like managers. It's a
waste of time, it's illusion, it's false pride, and it's an insult to the
complex, experienced, and talented managers (read: everybody
else) who work for us.

Perhaps a different way of describing the problem is that
organizations aren't really overmanaged and underled; rather,
the problem is that the leaders are trying to manage and the
managers don't know that they are supposed to. In the final analysis, micro-management isn't management at all. It's the red her-
ring of leadership. And the death of true self-management.

Using the "Load/Burden" Model

The key question we should ask when looking at the placement
of power in a given situation is whether we should retain the
power or share it. One way to frame this question is based on an
old concept of carrying a weight.

There are some things that people not only can, but also
should, do for themselves. They need to carry their own loads.
They might not be ready or willing to carry them, but they need
to do it anyway, because it's the right, responsible, and most
effective action to take.

There are other assignments that people just can't handle
by themselves, no matter how hard they try or how much they
want to. These assignments aren't loads, they're *burdens.* People
can't do these tasks alone, and it isn't fair or reasonable to ask

them (or worse, order them) to try. We need to help them carry these burdens, or help them to get the assistance required to do it. "I sit on a man's back choking him and making him carry me, and yet assure myself and others that I am very sorry for him and wish to lighten his load by all possible means—except by getting off his back," said Russian author Tolstoy.

The crucial question to ask is: "Is this a load they ought to be able to carry on their own, or is this a burden?" Answering the questions in Exhibit 8-1 can help us decide.

If your answers to any of these questions is a clear yes, then the assignment to others would likely be a burden. We need to retain or piecemeal the assignment, acquire for ourselves or the team the power to do it, and use our authority to make sure no part of the team is being asked to carry a burden instead of a load. If all your answers are no, on the other hand, the project is a load. We need to give the parties concerned the assignment, powershare with them, and use our authority to clear away the obstacles.

If we still have concerns or questions about powersharing, we can ask ourselves a second set of questions, shown in Exhibit 8-2. Unless you get a clear no to these questions, go ahead and powershare.

If, whenever we need to make an assignment or allocate power, we ask whether the project is a load or a burden and then take the time to answer these questions related to the individual or team that is sitting in front of us, we will move our leadership into the effective regions of balanced power.

Steps in Balancing the Quantity of Power

There are a number of things we can do to ensure the possibility of a truly interdependent organization. This can only come about, with all its attendant rewards, if we approximate the balancing of retaining and sharing power throughout our organization (or the piece of it for which we're responsible). Here are nine steps to take toward achieving that balance.

Exhibit 8-1. Questions to ask when deciding whether an
assignment is a burden.

Question	Yes	No	Unsure
1. Does this issue relate closely to the development, acceptance, implementation, or modification of our vision?			
2. Does this issue relate to strategic thinking (what do we do better than anyone else and whether anyone cares) versus strategic planning?			
3. Does this issue relate to organization-wide or long-term expectations or priorities?			
4. Does this issue involve key hiring, assignment, promotion, team membership, or team leadership decisions?			
5. Does this issue relate to the establishment, utilization, effectiveness, or modification of our system of positive and negative consequences?			
6. Does this issue involve a major crossroad or potential turning point, such as a large or unusual opportunity, an organization-wide crisis, or a significant and intractable problem?			
7. Is this an opportunity to reignite and inspire our people in a deep and fundamental way?			
8. Is this a situation where, regardless of the pressure to make a decision, I strongly believe that taking action is of questionable value or potentially harmful?			
9. Does this assignment play more to the recipient's weaknesses than to his strengths?			

Exhibit 8-2. Follow-up questions to ask when deciding whether to powershare.

Question	Yes	No	Unsure	N/A
1. Is anyone better equipped than I am to lead this effort or make this decision?				
2. Is the risk of harm to the organization small or at least reasonable acceptable?				
3. Is this an opportunity for one or more people to advance significantly in skills, knowledge, or wisdom?				
4. Is my reticence more related to personal feelings of diminishment or insecurity than to actual concerns about the effort?				
5. Do others have more time and/ or interest than I do in the nuances of this decision?				
6. Will morale be significantly improved by powersharing?				
7. Is powersharing likely to produce new ideas, perspectives, or solutions?				
8. Is powersharing more likely to get a response of gratitude than resentment?				
9. Am I sure that I'm not just dumping confusion, unsolvable problems, or no-win situations onto others?				

Step 1: Understand the Difference Between Leaders and Managers

This is an indispensable starting point. We truly have to grasp and believe in what was said earlier in this chapter about the differences between leading and managing. It means, further, that we have to spend part of our time as leaders being servants and another part being followers. In fact, leaders have several very different roles to play, in different mixes and percentages at different times. For instance, they have to be:

• *Visionary.* Leaders must live in the future and then come back and describe their vision.

• *Tone-setter.* Leaders must set the tone for the organization through their words, actions, and effective self-management.

• *Servants.* Leaders must be servants, clearing obstacles out of the way of their people that no one else has the power to do and ensuring that their people are deriving pleasure from their work.

• *Followers.* Leaders must know when others know more than they do and provide whatever help is necessary to such people. "In the complex interdependent reality we now inhabit, our self-interest—indeed our survival—demands that we become as adept at following others as we are at getting them to follow us. . . . performance challenges—not position—should determine when you should follow and when you should lead."[2]

Step 2: Understand Our Relationship With Power

Our power is an amorphous entity, hard to define and even harder to use wisely. We've already seen that we have to give up the idea that we can use our power to manage and control. Even if we could manage, we shouldn't, because it's a waste of our talent and a low-value use of our power.

We increase our power—our authority—by leading, and we diminish it by managing. It might appear that our power is increased when we try to manage others, but that is truly an illusion. The ship is heading toward the wrong port while we debate the nuances of instrument usage with the navigator. We may even be able to get the navigator to agree to talk about it and do it our way even if she knows that we're wrong. That can *feel* like power. It can *look* like power. And so it is. Destructive power.

Perhaps another way of saying this is that our power *is* increased when we use it to manage others. But it's an increase in the wrong kind of power.

But power shared—with self-managers—is power multiplied.

Step 3: Know What We Must Do With Our Power

The leader is sometimes a social architect.

To reach the higher regions of success as a leader, we have to use our power to design. We have to become organizational architects.

The greatest and best use of a leader's authority is to implement a comprehensive design, using the principle of "form follows function." First, we have to determine the function of the organization, the whole organization or whatever piece of it is under our authority. The function, the *raison d'être,* is the vision. Where is this ship going? Why should we care? Why should anybody care?

The hard part, the trick, of leadership is clearly defining the function. "It has to do with the ability to lay out difficult issues in a balanced and clear way," explains Peter Senge. "The simple goal, no more, no less, is to elevate the quality of thinking and the quality of discourse. . . . corporate leaders are being asked to do [this] and they're having difficulty because they're not particularly skilled or competent at it."[3]

Then we can move to the design of form, the structure that will support the function (the vision). The trick is to remember that form *follows* function. Too many departments, plants, stores, and entire organizations have their form designed before the function is determined or, in the worst cases, in lieu of the function.

Because of the need today for innovation, flexible response, and massive multilevel communication, a form that will most likely be superior in many applications in the coming years is the open, connected organization with some level of internal market economy (with the possible exceptions of the military and—my personal vote—the drive-through operations in fast-food restaurants). How can we share power with people if they're living in a closed, centralized, hierarchical organization?

We need a free market inside the organization for power-sharing to achieve what it promises. The form of the organization should also include a constitution based on the rule of law and enduring principles, supported by an internal justice system. The form needs a lot of freedom—and a Bill of Rights, too, so that people won't be imprisoned (frozen in the organization) or executed (terminated) without due process.

Finally, the form needs to replace the static, rigidifying, mostly inaccurate world of job descriptions with a dynamic, demanding, and clear world of job *expectations,* which focus on results and goals rather than duties and responsibilities.

In short, we can't powershare with people in organizations in which there is no clear function (vision) or form (reasonable systems based on principles rather than lists of rules and detailed policy/procedure manuals).

Step 4: Accept the Limits of Power

Everything has limits, including our power. Whether we acknowledge them or illude that they don't exist or don't apply to us are choices that will determine whether we will be successful and admired or unsuccessful (even if we make a lot of money) and loathed.

First and most important, we must accept the fact that we can't force our organization to be successful. We can force it to do many things; it's just that being successful isn't one of them. Most new leaders fall into the trap of beginning their exercise of power *out there,* using it on people, flexing their muscles to make the organization "ooh" and "aah." Kick some behind. Shake things up. Make things happen.

But this is both the wrong and the ineffective place to start. We have to begin (and just about end) by using our power on ourselves. "Those who wish to transform the world must be able to transform themselves," said German historian Konrad Heiden. We have to use our power to create a strong personal identity with a clear and consistent vision (personal and organizational) over time. It's *character* (power turned inward to create a self of integrity and intensity) and not control (power turned outward in a display of force and ferocity) that moves organizations to the highest heights.

Then we can pick clear and simple ways, perhaps by the use of stories or the "spin" we put on incidents, to convey our vision to those with whom we have powershared.

Because our power is limited by our own strengths and weaknesses, a good rule to follow throughout the organization is to do the assignments that fall within our areas of strength and to delegate those that lie in our areas of weakness. For example, we can let someone else handle a sensitive negotiation if our communication or diplomatic skills are weak, or ask someone else to lead the proposal presentation to a client if our platform skills are minimal. This puts our power where we can be the most effective, probably in part because it's where we are most interested.

There you have it. Our power is largely limited to who we are and, scary thought, *by* who we are. And are choosing to become.

Step 5: Understand Personal Weaknesses That Lead to Misplaced Powersharing

We have to really understand ourselves if we're going to balance our authority with powersharing.

Some of us tend to be overresponsible. We feel responsible for everybody and everything. If things don't go well, we feel guilty and ashamed, as if we've let somebody down. If other people aren't doing well, we can become professional rescuers, riding in like the Lone Ranger, jumping to make it all better, stretching ourselves thin and limiting people's opportunity to learn from mistakes and confusion. If this is our approach, we're going to cling to power, define power as control, destroy our leadership by becoming managers, and pull power out of the organization at the earliest opportunities.

Others of us tend to be underresponsible. If things don't go well, we feel uninvolved or angry, as if others have let us down. If other people aren't doing well, we can become professional scapegoaters, riding in like the posse, jumping all over people, stretching our people thin and limiting our collective opportunity to learn from mistakes and confusion. If this is our approach, we're going to dump power, define power as the ability to fix the blame, destroy our leadership by avoiding self-management, and pull power out of the organization after it's been misused or abused and we have delegated the appropriate blame.

Some of us, sadly, waver back and forth between the two. We hold on to everything, get burned out and frustrated with the noninvolvement of our people, then start pushing power at them whether or not they're ready for it. Then, when they flop, we blame them and the "empowerment thing" and pull the power back into our domain. Back and forth the pendulum can swing, over-responsible to underresponsible, control to laissez-faire, managing to scapegoating.

The seeds of many of our personal weaknesses go deep into the nature of who we are and back to the early stages of our life journeys. We have to try to understand what these drivers are so that we can compensate for them and take the necessary steps to achieve a balance of power in spite of our imperfections. Personality and other useful tests can help us get to know ourselves. But we're also going to have to do some deep work, some soul sweat, if we're going to understand ourselves well enough to be able to balance power realistically and effectively.[4]

Step 6: Accept the Limits of Powersharing

We have to understand that powersharing is no "grand" solution to our problems. Some of the trendiest management literature implies that this is the magic pill, when it is not. Or perhaps it *is* magic, a drug that promises wonderful results but doesn't advertise that it might be laced with arsenic.

The success of powersharing is limited by the education, training, expertise, experience, interest, commitment, personality, strengths, weaknesses, motives, values, ideals, and rottennesses of those with whom we powershare. It's also limited by the fact that sometimes it is necessary for us or someone else to retain power and exercise authority.

Also, people who should be allowed to exercise power in one situation or circumstance or assignment might be disastrous repositories of power in a different setting.

Balancing power is an exercise in fluidity. We can't design the perfect powersharing system, put it in place, and then sit back and watch the machine hum. There *is* no powersharing "system." "Participative styles of management create more innovation, initiative, and commitment, but also more unpredictable behavior," says author Stephen Covey.[5]

Powersharing is partly strategic and rational but mainly situational and intuitive. The criteria in Chapters 6 and 7 can guide us. Judgment based on wisdom, and not decisions based on data, is the key to victory here.

Step 7: Review the Reality With Our Followers

When we begin to talk with our people about sharing and retaining power (and we have to talk about both), we need to review the reality of what these concepts are and what they aren't, based on what we're discussing in this book.

Some of the people will be predisposed to interpret powersharing as a new "fad." Our plans will be immediately discounted.

Others will be predisposed to translate it as a "dump" of management's (*er,* leadership's) responsibility onto them. We can almost hear the wheels of "it's not my job" thinking turning in the audience.

Still others will be predisposed to believe that "freedom has come at last." Plots to aggrandize power and use it for personal and turf-building ends will hatch before we've finished speaking.

No effective interdependence, no balancing of power, will occur without a vast quantity of dialogue and a lot of time. We have to "sell" what the balance is frequently and repetitively, and we have to listen to what our people are saying back to us. Maintaining a balance of power depends on a deep understanding of, and effective use of, dialogue. We have to measure the impact of our ideas and balancing efforts and carefully build in the balance of power, perhaps in stages rather than all at once.

Step 8: Look for the Clues to Insufficient Powersharing

There are some clues that might be telling us that we have retained too much power, as, for instance, when:

- We spend more than 5 to 10 percent of our time fighting fires.
- We spend more than 5 percent of our time answering detailed questions.
- We spend more than 10 to 15 percent of our time making decisions (or make more than 10 to 15 percent of the decisions).
- We find ourselves saying no frequently.
- We get little in the way of creativity, initiative, recommendations, or suggestions from our people.
- We have high turnover or poor morale among the best people.

Step 9: Expose Ourselves to Interdependent Cultures

It's hard to become something that we've never seen modeled.

We've got to find ways to experience firsthand what an interdependent culture looks and feels like. Attendance at seminars, reading of books, discussions with colleagues at trade meetings, plant visits—we've got to take advantage of every opportunity to experience interdependence in action.

When we do, we've also got to make an evaluation of where they are in the process of building interdependence. A fledgling effort is going to look a lot different from a finely tuned operation. Only when we've made this analysis can we clearly see how to bring interdependence into our organization, and at what level, and how fast.

Notes

1. Caela Farren and Beverly L. Kaye, "New Skills for New Leadership Roles," in *The Leader of the Future: New Visions, Strategies, and Practices for the Next Era* (San Francisco: Jossey-Bass, 1996), p. 177.
2. Douglas K. Smith, "The Following Part of Leading," in *The Leader of The Future*, p. 204.
3. Peter Senge, as quoted in *USA Today*, 26 August 1996, p. 3B.
4. For more help in doing this, see Chapter 17, "Soul Sweat:

Winning by Facing the Truth," in my book *Fatal Illusions: Shredding a Dozen Unrealities That Can Keep Your Organization From Success* (New York: AMACOM, 1997).
5. Stephen R. Covey, *Principle-Centered Leadership* (New York: Simon & Schuster, 1991), p. 184.

9

Conquering the Factors That Breed Dependence

> We have witnessed in modern business the submergence of the individual within the organization, and yet the increase of an extraordinary degree of the power . . . of the individual who happens to control the organization. Most men are individual no longer so far as their business, its activities, or its moralities are concerned. They are not units but fractions.
>
> —Woodrow Wilson

Since having a proper balance of power will be one of the most critical organizational assets in the years to come, let's take a close look at some factors that can either bring dependence into an organization or expand what's already there.

We'll begin by looking at those factors that produce dependence in individuals. Then we'll turn our sights on the crippling dependence-building factors at work in teams.

The Factors That Breed Dependence in Individuals

At least ten factors can work to create dependence in the individuals who work for organizations.

Laziness

Life is just plain hard.

There's no way around it. There are moments of grand joy and ease or even leisure, but sooner or later we've got to admit that a lot of life is just plain hard. Just getting up, day after day, getting ready, going to work, dealing with routine, dealing with baloney, can take its toll. We can start looking for a way to make things easier. This is fine if we're talking about faster or better ways of doing things.

The problem comes when we just don't want to do what we're supposed to be doing at all. Our creativity dies and we fall into doing what's "expected," what we're told to do. We become dependent on others to set our agendas and push us into action.

Suggested Solution: Never let people get too comfortable. Hit them with new ideas, new tools, new ways. Challenge them with books and articles that suggest that the way we're doing things is stupid or out of date. Send them to seminars. Have them *teach* a seminar. Rotate them; we need to be uncomfortable with allowing anyone to remain in the exact same role for more than three to five years. What about "experience"? you ask. Doing the same thing over and over for twenty-five years isn't "experience"; it's punishment, the organizational equivalent of making license plates. A good indication that we've established the right amount of challenge is when people are good at their work, the atmosphere is charged with energy, and nobody feels as if they've "got it all together."

Entitlement Thinking

At times, it seems that the whole thrust of organizational life, at least in the later stages of the industrial revolution, has been that "the organization will take care of you."

There is something in human nature that wants to shun personal or collective responsibility and be "taken care of." If the truth be told, we see this pattern at play throughout history as people willingly give up their personal freedom and even basic human rights so that somebody else will do their thinking and planning for them. From the serfs in feudal times to the peoples who in the twentieth century have yielded to dictators out of fear of chaos, history is full of the results of this desire to be a dependent of . . . somebody.

And there is the other side, the part of human nature that wants to take care of others (which can be altruistic and good) and make them dependent on us (which is narcissistic and bad).

In the life of the modern organization, these two unhealthy desires—the desire to be dependent and the desire to make others dependent—have found a warm home.

The result is "entitlement thinking" all around. Those who are dependent come to feel that they have a "right" to be dependent and to have their needs met. They think they are entitled not to have to think about profit and loss, product or service viability, long-range plans, or the impact of their performance (good or bad) on the health of the organization. When pay and benefits have to be restrained or cut, the wails go up: "Wait a minute, we're entitled to those things." And when demands for individuals to take more responsibility and have more accountability for results are made, the wails go up again: "That's management's job, not mine."

But the entitlement mentality lives in the minds of those on top as well. In a dependent culture, those in authority come to feel that they have a "right" (divine right of kings?) to do all of the thinking, make all of the decisions, and take most of the money. They believe they're entitled to respect, whether they've earned it or not, and to a positive response from their dependents ("They should be happy to have a job"). It's too easy for the mental model to be "You people owe me your life" and to believe that we're entitled to their gratitude.

Suggested Solution: Let people know in no uncertain terms that we don't owe them a living, but also broadcast the equally new message that we do owe them a chance to be fully human, to take responsibility, to think and plan for themselves, to be accountable, to own up to mistakes and learn from them, to grow, and to be rewarded on the basis of the results they achieve. We can urge people to act as though they are in business for themselves, to develop a (personal) business plan, to treat others like customers, to enhance their skills. And we can establish a reward and recognition system that rewards results rather than existence.

Followership Orientation

Almost any time people gather together, at work or elsewhere, you can see this orientation in action. Somebody begins to dominate the time, the conversation, and the ideas. And others let them.

This isn't just because some people have strong personalities or even because they're domineering. It's because most people are willing—even wanting—to be followers, at least in certain situations or areas of their lives. Even those with great authority can fall victim to this way of thinking, as evidenced by U.S. presidents—ostensibly the most powerful men in the world—who have become the most spineless of followers in their reverence for and adherence to the "leadership" of opinion polls. They wouldn't be elected otherwise, many people say; but maybe we ought to elect an "unelectable" candidate who really believes in something besides electability.

We're trained to do this "following" thing from birth on. "Follow directions," "follow the rules," "follow my example," "follow the crowd," "follow the styles." Find out what's going on, and follow along with it. But what if the directions don't make sense, the rules are pointless, the example is bad, the crowd is wrong, and we hate the styles? We're all born unique, yet most people die as carbon copies.

Suggested Solution: Insist that people think for themselves. Make "tell me three new ideas about what we should be doing around here" a key component of every performance evaluation you conduct. Reward and recognize people who don't follow directions, rules, examples, or anything else when these things are wrong (that is, unethical or harmful) or ineffective (that is, not adding value to stakeholders or wasteful). If we're going to do this, we'll have to agree in broad terms on what *wrong* and *ineffective* mean. And we have to be prepared to deal with people who don't agree or don't want to do it our way. Make sure that all employees "lead" at least one project or team at least once a year, on topics that force them to imagine a bigger world than they already know. Give lots of trust to those who show themselves to be completely honest, and relieve them of some of their routine accountability reporting.

Lack of Commitment to Employer

Lack of commitment leads to uninvolvement with the success or failure of the organization. Curiously, this leads to even greater dependence, as "magical thinking" takes over. It's the same kind of idea had by students who aren't really committed to their education and don't study, but hope that somehow they'll get a good grade anyway. The thinking is, "I don't know where we're heading, and I don't really care, but if I keep my head down and stay out of trouble it'll work out for me."

Commitment is different from loyalty, which we discussed in Chapter 2. We can reasonably expect commitment to entail more than just "doing my job." There can be commitment to a strong, compelling vision that connects with people's personal goals. But expecting loyalty, a "my company right or wrong" attitude, is in many ways a quest for the Holy Grail. We probably have no employees who wouldn't quit tomorrow if they inherited millions (and if they didn't quit, they're either the most devoted people we've got or lunatics who don't have a life outside of work). Loyalty is a treasure that is given to leaders here or there based on the development of strong personal ties; it can't be duplicated or mass-produced throughout an organization. Commitment, on the other hand, is a reasonable expectation that can be "mass-produced," given the right "productive" environment.

Suggested Solution: Frankly, many employers in my experience don't deserve any commitment, in large part because they don't give any. If we want commitment *from* our people, we've got to start by making commitments *to* them. We can reasonably commit ourselves to helping people be continuous learners, giving them a safe and healthy environment to work in, assisting them in developing their skills and careers, providing them with varied and (if earned) increasing opportunities, keeping them informed, and treating them with justice and equity. In return, we can ask them to commit themselves to learning, to adding to the environment, to developing themselves, to making the most of their opportunities, to using the information we give them while keeping us informed in return, and to treating us and their colleagues with justice and equity.

And if, here or there in a lifetime, we find a few individuals willing to give us their loyalty, we'd better fight hard to keep it.

Lack of Passion About the Work to Be Done

It should go without saying, but it doesn't, so I'll say it: People aren't going to do well at something they do unhappily.

I *hate* it when I see people going through the motions. And it doesn't just occur in blue-collar or entry-level jobs. I've seen top executives who have lost the "fire in the belly," and I've seen people making minimum wage in service businesses who care and shine and create a positive experience for the customer.

Lack of passion can come from narrow causes (for example, we've got the wrong person in the job, his personality doesn't fit) or broad causes (we've created a boring culture, our teams are poorly structured). But make no mistake about it: The absence of passion is a precursor of the absence of organizational viability. It causes people to be dependent on the form of their job because they bring nothing new of value to it.

Suggested Solution: We've got to get the right people in each area of effort. This means that we've got to look first at what people are interested in and think is important, and only then at their education and experience. It's a lot easier to train the impassioned than to impassion the trained. We need to take off the straightjackets and put people where they're excited to be. We have to understand what's driving them, even if it never shows up on their résumé. And we have to create a guiding vision that people can get excited about, which means that we have to involve them in its development and ask their opinion, not just about whether they agree but about whether they're fired up about it.

And then we'll have to change all of the above at different times, because variety really is the spice of life.

Lack of Training

If people don't know what to do, they're going to wait to be told
what to do—and how to do it. Dependence thrives.

Some people will wait longer than others. Based on the distribution of personality types in the culture, it's safe to say that
the majority of people will wait and delay and procrastinate and
expect us to "do something" when they don't have enough training, information, or tools to do the job.

Suggested Solution: We shouldn't *give* people training.
That very thought is dependency-producing. We need to make
people responsible for their own training. Our role is to help
them see where they need to be, where they are now, and what
resources are available to them to close the gap. Then we should
make this closure part of their performance agreement/evalua-
tion. We also need to offer people counterintuitive training to
get them out of their ruts. Training outside the field is every bit
as important as job-related training. So many organizations reim-
burse employees only for "job-related" courses. What *isn't* job-
related? What a strategic planner learns in a history course on
the Middle Ages might make the difference for us in the age to
come.

Training is the great underestimated tool of leadership. "A
10 percent increase in employees' average education yielded an
8.6 percent increase in output. In comparison, a 10 percent increase in capital investment (tools, buildings, and machinery)
produced only a 3.4 percent increase in productivity," a Census
Bureau study found.[1] Worse than training people and losing
them is *not* training them and keeping them.

Difficulty in Developing Innovative Ideas

So many of us were trained to believe that we don't have much
to offer. It's hard to believe that our ideas have value.

It's amazing that as children we have such a high level of
both creativity and confidence, and yet by the time we're adults
(often, long before) we've had those assets trained and beaten
right out of us. How many "that's stupid" (or worse, "you're
stupid") comments do we have to hear before we learn the les-

son that we'll be better off keeping our opinions to ourselves? This can cause us to be dependent on others for information, ideas, approvals, or blessings.

Suggested Solution: Put people into "what if" situations that will force them to be creative. Get everyone involved in brainstorming—on small issues at first to give them practice, and then graduate them to the bigger ones. Insist that everyone take sabbaticals, periods of rest during which we ask them to think about a few big-picture, out-of-the-ordinary issues important to our organization. These sabbaticals can work to stir thought and rid people of their parasitical clinging to the organization if we give them a short agenda with a long expectation for suggestions. The time away could last a few days every year (on the company's nickel) and from sixty to ninety days every seven years with a bigger agenda and an even longer list of expectations for suggestions. These should also be at the company's expense (or at least the costs should be split, if we want them to make an investment in themselves as well). What? How can we afford that? The real question to ask is, how can we *not* afford the difference between a mentally and emotionally dead person and a living, breathing dynamo?[2]

Self-Contempt

All too many people believe that they have no value. They blame themselves for everything. Some even believe that they have no right to exist. To compensate for their perceived lack of value, they can attach themselves to somebody or something else (including our organization or us as strong leaders) where they can find value in association, in co-opting our identity. They're depending on us to give them value. That is why so many people, when we ask them to tell us about themselves, start by saying "I work for . . ." rather than "I'm pretty creative. . . ." Their very neediness can lead to choking, even parasitical dependence. People in this dependence-for-value mode can become dangerous when we don't give them the "value" they're expecting (we can't), and they can easily and quickly convert their self-contempt into contempt for us or our organization. They might follow us around like puppy dogs right up to the moment that they turn into raging pit bulls.

We can't solve the problems of the world. Some people are too "broken" for us to effectively employ until they've taken some steps toward personal growth. But the majority of people probably carry around some measure of self-contempt, and the majority of them can probably be helped past it to some degree.

Suggested Solution: We have to explore in depth during interviews how people have contributed to their past organizations and how they felt about their contributions and those organizations. We can listen for the sounds of self-contempt ("I did the best I could," "I was surprised they gave me so much responsibility") or other-centered contempt ("Those people really let me down," "They expected too much"), and avoid hiring them if the sounds get too loud.

Once hired, people have to be nurtured to believe that they have value and that their opinions, especially if they train themselves and live as continuous learners, have value as well. We must also ensure that the leaders in the organization don't use their power unjustly to batter people's egos and strip them of their self-confidence—a true abuse of power, an organizational felony. We need to stand up for our people in the face of onslaughts by those in high positions of formal authority. And believe, with Malcom X, that "Power in defense of freedom is greater than power in behalf of tyranny and oppression."[3]

We will bring out emotional interconnections in our followers because everyone has needs, and some of those needs we can meet. We just have to make sure that it is *we* who determine what needs we are able and willing to meet, and not be drawn into crippling, dysfunctional attachments inadvertently—or because it feels good to be "needed."

Resistance to the Stress of Responsibility

All responsibility—from caring for the newborn through assisting the college student, from the responsibilities of a first job to those of a leadership position, from paying the utility bills to buying a house—brings stress.

The problem comes when the responsibility is more than

we can handle and the stress becomes too great. Stress is a true test and measure of character, and it's all too easy to fail the test. Stress often drives us as human beings to the point of seeking relief, often in things we can "depend" on to be there, like alcohol, drugs, food, spending, a person, or an organization.

An overemphasis on personal accountability can bring on this feeling of massive stress and resultant dependency. "If the Japanese understand one thing about collegial power (and they understand many)," Robert Dilenschneider writes, "it is that risk must be shared rather than forced down as individual accountability."[4] Not everything is some*one's* responsibility; some things belong to a number of us (such as a project or new product development), some things belong to all of us (for instance, the systems or culture), and some things belong to none of us (for example, customers who decide to provide our service for themselves). Interdependent leaders learn to distinguish among these.

Suggested Solution: Two of our top priorities must be the following: first, delegating responsibility and expecting accountability from the right levels (individuals, teams, departments, and so on) so that we are not placing a burden where only a load should be carried; and second, controlling the stress levels in our organizations. A certain level of pressure, if it's not continual but has some ebb and flow, can be creativity-producing. At another level, pressure becomes stress and is always crippling and dependency-producing. Excellent leaders learn how to relieve, as well as how to apply, pressure.

Fear of Consequences

Fear of consequences can drive people to look for a refuge or a way out. Dependency ("You won't abandon me when I fail, will you?") can provide both a refuge and a way out. It appears to provide assurances and security in spite of willful poor performance.

As leaders, we have to distinguish between legitimate and illegitimate consequences. Legitimate consequences can be both positive and negative. They are reasonable, fair, in proportion to the related action, and sprinkled with mercy and understanding.

They could include incentive plans at one end of the continuum and a disciplinary policy at the other. Illegitimate consequences are arbitrary, unrelated in form or size to the action that sparked them, and sprinkled with harshness and confusion. Examples of illegitimate consequences are verbal and emotional abuse, chastisement for honest mistakes, the silent treatment, and ostracism. People rightly fear these results, and, in the upside-down world of co-dependency, become more seriously enmeshed with their abusers.

If we say that our people have power but they're afraid of illegitimate consequences, whatever else they have they do *not* have power.

Suggested Solution: If people fear legitimate consequences, in a certain sense it's okay. This is one of the reasons to *have* legitimate consequences. If they are paralyzed by this fear, it's a personal responsibility issue; we'll need to include consequences for inaction as well as action. And we'll need to counter the fear with greater powersharing (including helping people to realize and utilize the power they already have), clarity about their ownership of the problem, a stronger sense of the importance of their relationship to us, and more practice in self-discipline so that they can avoid the negative legitimate consequences.

If they fear illegitimate consequences, there are two steps. First, we have to make sure that their fear itself isn't illegitimate (that is, the alleged consequences exist only in their heads, not in reality). And second, we have to correct or discard any truly illegitimate consequences that are cluttering up our leadership library.

The Factors That Breed Dependence in Teams

Teams can become millstones and drags on organizational performance if they sink to a dependent level. The total can easily become less than the sum of its parts. A lot of time and effort can be expended forming teams, holding meetings, and producing reports, but an impotent team will produce nothing new or valuable.

When teams, with all their promise, stagnate, it's worse than if we'd never introduced the team concept at all. People already battle feelings of disempowerment in most organizations. When we collect them together and *still* nothing happens, the feelings of helplessness and worthlessness can be paralyzing.

For leaders, a dependent team is a double drag: first, it consumes a lot of our time in maintenance; and second, it can become an obstacle to getting things done, a veto by simply being in the way.

Let's take a look at some factors that can produce an energyless, dependent team.

The Tendency of People to Defer to Strong Personalities

Whether at a small social gathering or a large meeting of executives, it's amazing how fast a pecking order of power can develop.

In general, people tend to regress in a group. This regression can be to a followership role, even if the person is normally a leader in her own sphere of influence. The regression can go further back to a childlike state, depending on the weaknesses in our own character and the strength or dominance of others in the group. The regression is always magnified as the strength of other personalities in the group is perceived to be greater. We defer to these people on the basis of the power they project—according to their status, knowledge, or self-confidence.

The problem is, of course, that the team can simply become a sounding board and rubber stamp for the dominant personality. Nothing new is really contributed, because most of the members are merely following someone else's lead.

Suggested Solution: We should seldom, if ever, put dominant personalities in formal charge of a team. When this type of personality is combined with the additional power of designated team leadership, the role of other team members can fade away. We also shouldn't put the weakest member in charge, because he won't have the power to keep the dominant personalities focused, and we'll end up with the dominant person being the de facto leader. We need to have team leaders who themselves are balanced between willingness to lead and willingness to follow, and who are able to balance the power of the team along the same lines on a continual basis. They have to be "strong" enough to lead the team and "weak" enough to drain every last ounce of creativity out of each team member.

We can also teach our people about team/group dynamics and the tendency of people to regress. Once they see and understand this phenomenon, they can catch themselves and others when they find themselves doing it.

Imbalance in Contributions of Team Members

Why have someone on a team if she isn't going to contribute anything? Just so we can say "everyone here is on a team"?

All noncontributors do is to dissipate the energy, passion, and creativity of the team. Even if they aren't verbally negative, their lack of interest and involvement will come through in their facial expressions and body language. The team can severely limit itself by expending vast amounts of energy trying to "draw them out," and the level of team output can fall to the lowest common denominator. Who needs that?

Suggested Solution: We can make team membership a privilege rather than a right. We can take steps to ensure that continued membership on this or other teams is based on a person's contribution to the results of the team and on nothing else. And we can vary the rewards and recognition of team members so that those who contribute the most get the most; perhaps we could have a common "team portion" of the reward/recognition that's the same for all members and then an "individual portion" that relates to personal contribution. We can use the input of the team members themselves to help us determine who the contributors are. Level of contribution to teams can also be made a substantial portion of an employee's performance evaluation. If someone is uncomfortable contributing for correctable reasons (for example, they're new to the language or they lack training in presentation skills), we should take the necessary steps to remove these barriers.

We can also work to ensure that there is a diversity of personalities on the team (for example, by including people on the team who are personally committed to involving everyone and who will work to draw the quiet ones out of their closet). And always include on the team a strong person who knows little or nothing about the problem or issue at hand. Not only will she shake up the conversation, but her example can show everyone that it's all right to question and disagree.

A rotating "illusion shredder" can help to get alternative opinions on the table. For each meeting or series of meetings, assign a different person to take this role, and let everyone else on the team know what the role is and who is taking it. An expectation that someone will be contrary *by design* can draw people into the conversation and generate some show-stopping ideas.

Unhealthy Criticism

Unhealthy criticism is criticism that tears down without offering an alternative building plan. It attacks ideas in their infancy, assaults proposals that are different from our own or different from the way things have always been done, and often rips up suggestions that have been presented by someone who is perceived to be a personal threat.

Unhealthy criticism can come from either outside or inside the team. Unhealthy criticism from the outside is at times more crippling and dependency-producing. When team output is criticized constantly by those in formal authority, team members become tentative. They curtail the pursuit of ideas that attract the most criticism, and begin listening for clues about what the authorities want to hear. Internal criticism can have the same effect, especially if it comes from a strong personality.

Suggested Solution: We have to emphasize to our team leaders that one of their primary roles, perhaps the most important, is to protect the team and its members from unhealthy criticism (but *not* from the truth). They have to make wise decisions about when to share outside criticism with the team, if at all, and they have to keep a tight rein over criticism given within the group. In general, criticism from team members should be stated in a positive, nonadversarial manner and should always be accompanied by suggested alternatives. We as leaders will have to work hard to keep much of our criticism to ourselves, at least until the proper time and place.

Hierarchical Organizational Structure

A little hierarchy might not be a bad thing. Too much can demolish initiative.

Crippling hierarchy can come into the picture from outside or inside the team. Outside damage can occur if the team does not truly have power, if it can make no important decisions, change no directions, spend no money. These restrictions change the team into a "suggestion committee," which is a much less effective life form than a team that truly has power. The hierarchy can also be internal when a "caste" system develops in which different members are accorded different levels of attention and respect, or one member without whom nothing can be decided becomes the de facto dictator.

Suggested Solution: After the team and its operating guidelines (*general* operating guidelines) are established, the organizational hierarchy needs to disappear. Its presence will almost always stifle initiative, accountability, and the taking of responsibility. Better than a list of what the team can do or decide or spend is a *short* list of what the team can't do (like spend more than we have in the bank, burn down headquarters, or assassinate authority figures).

Within the team, it must be understood and agreed that no member is more important than any other, except by personal choice through ongoing contribution, and that no member is important enough to stop the progress of the team by his absence. And we can consider making a certain number of unexcused absences grounds for removal from the team.

Fear of Being Open About Ideas and Assumptions

Fear and dependency go hand in hand.

When we're afraid, we begin to look for ways to protect ourselves. The "way" often turns out to be someone else (such as someone in top management, a team leader, a strong fellow team member) who, for our allegiance, agrees to "protect" us. At its most extreme stage—as is seen so often in homes rife with alcohol, drugs, and violence—it can become dependency on the very ones who are making us afraid. In organizations worldwide, thousands of otherwise competent people are converted by fear into bootlicking the ones who are scaring them to death. It's a "protection racket": The neighborhood criminals sell us "protection" from themselves for a price, and the "neighborhood" organizational leaders do the same. The price? Loss of our humanity.

Most of us have learned the hard way that being vulnerable can be an invitation to being harmed. This problem—that people will use our openness against us—is so prevalent a part of the human condition that, if thought about long enough, it can cause us to forswear ever saying what's on our minds again.

Suggested Solution: Edwards Deming said it—we have to drive fear from the workplace—but few organizations have really done it. Fear turns people into craven slaves and intellectual hermits. We have to evaluate team leaders and others in authority on their ability to drive fear out and not introduce any new fear of their own. We'll need to ask their team members and colleagues how they're doing on this score (and how *we're* doing). And we'll have to fight ferociously to get battle-hardened people to expose their ideas and underlying assumptions, and to criminalize any words or actions that drive them back into hiding.

"No fear" shouldn't be just a statement of attitude and courage. It should also be a statement of organizational purpose.

Lack of Diverse Sources of Information

One of the worst jokes in organizational life is the "self-managed team" that knows only what those in authority think necessary to tell it.

As individuals, we can turn encounters with others into pure illusion. We often present only what we want them to see or perceive. One of the giant shortcomings of counseling, therapy, and analysis is that the expert hears only one side—the client's side. Most of the client's problems relate to others, but the analyst never sees him or her interact with others, and seldom talks with those others to get a more complete and balanced perspective. Even knowledgeable experts are dependent on the client's ability to tell the truth and, at an even deeper level, on the client's ability to *see* the truth.

Teams that get only "authorized" information are in the same dilemma as the therapist. How do we know that you're telling us the truth? How do we know that you even know what the truth is? Preselected information is certain to lead to predetermined decisions on the part of the team. We need to move away from the "when we want your opinion, we'll give it to you" path to team dependency.

Suggested Solution: Information is a tool of power. Powerful teams have access to many diverse sources of information, both inside and outside the organization. And they can access that information at times and in quantities of their own choosing. We need to encourage our teams to research widely and deeply, to look for information in odd places, to bring together information or knowledge from widely divergent fields, and to grab hold of and dissect the lone fact that is contrary to, and calls into question, our basic assumptions and directions.

Use of Discussion Rather Than Dialogue

Few teams, in my experience, get beyond the level of discussion, in which each person presents her position, the air fills with the sounds of debate, and a decision is made. This makes the team dependent on what it already knows, although what it "knows" might not even be true.

True dialogue is a linchpin of interdependency. Real, creative brainstorming is a powerful move away from dependency on the past, our limited views, and our mistaken assumptions. No team ever moves to interdependency without dialogue.

Suggested Solution: We need to train our teams in the principles of dialogue ("talking both ways"). These principles include the ability to refrain from restating existing opinions (which may be correct in some ways but are almost certainly imperfect and incomplete); a willingness to make the assumptions behind our thoughts and feelings transparent; an ability to "deeply listen" to others over an extended period of time; and an ability to ask probing questions that require narrative answers.

Teams often need conversation a lot more than they need debate.

Improper Emphasis on "Loyalty" and "Cooperation"

How we define concepts is critical to how we act on them.

If *loyalty* is defined as "toeing the organizational line" and "doing what you're told," we can give up on interdependency—and we can give up on teams at the same time. And if *cooperation* is defined as "not rocking the boat" or "getting along with others"—the triumph of harmony over progress—we have *institutionalized* dependency. "We must not confuse dissent with disloyalty," cautioned journalist Edward R. Murrow.

Suggested Solution: We need to define these words in interdependent terms and then live by those definitions. *Loyalty* then becomes "doing what's best for the organization even if it makes everybody madder than hell." And "cooperation" becomes "working closely with other complex, multifaceted beings to see if we can produce something of value without killing each other."

Who's more loyal, the team or team member who without protest lets us drive over the cliff? Or the one who screams at us until we hit the brakes? Who's more cooperative, the team or team member who eliminates the sparks by putting out the fire? Or the one who keeps the fire going until something gets cooked?

Not Holding Everyone Responsible for the Whole

One of the most de-energizing things a team can do is to not hold everyone on the team responsible for the results of the whole team.

Teams can go beyond dependency to actual destructiveness if individual members don't feel responsible for what the team does. In the words of Scott Peck, "Any group will remain inevitably potentially conscienceless and evil until such time as each and every individual holds himself or herself directly responsible for the behavior of the whole group . . . of which he or she is a part."[4] The death knell of team integrity sounds like this: "Hey, I did my part; don't blame me for what others did."

Suggested Solution: We have to truly believe in and reinforce the idea that before a team can be successful every member must feel responsible for ensuring that the team meets its goals. We have to let team members know that both success and failure accrue to everyone who takes part. This approach works best when people have some, or even a lot of, say over what teams they're on and who they'll team up with. We can help by establishing teams with varying levels of power, and then by making membership on the more powerful teams contingent upon success on lower-level teams. We could also have every member sign the team's mission statement or list of objectives.

Undefined or Unclear Expectations for the Team

In the absense of clearly defined and articulated expectations, the natural inclination of teams is to go slowly, stop frequently, and wait for orders from headquarters.

Why? There are few souls brave enough to move through unchartered territory. Without an incentive to do it, the effort becomes even less likely. Throw in the herd instinct, the desire not to break with the crowd, and the team actually becomes a *barrier* to even the few brave souls.

Suggested Solution: All teams, like all workers, should be self-managing. We can get so burdened with what the team is doing that we forget our role, which is to be concerned with where the team is going. We've got to focus on defining and articulating a reasonable (read: small) number of expectations. To be really effective, these expectations should be just beyond the reach of the current, combined capability of the individual members of the team. This will cause the team to have to work interdependently if it's going to meet the expectations.

●

We have seen that there are many ways to disempower people and strip them of their reason for existence. The role of those in authority, including team leaders, has to be delicately established and self-limited if those many ways are to be avoided.

At times it can be hard to find the balance or to believe that dependency is really so bad. People who want to be dependent on us can give us a thrill. It can feel good to be needed.

But somewhere, probably sooner rather than later, it will stop feeling good. It will feel more like a millstone around our necks. We'll come to resent their reactivity and inactivity. We'll feel burned out. And then we'll feel burned up. Our resentment will produce anger, but it won't kill the dependence.

But if we take the steps outlined in this chapter, we can really move our people toward interdependence.

Notes

1. From a 1995 study of 3,000 businesses by the University of Pennsylvania, conducted for the U.S. Census Bureau. As reported in *Training & Development Forum,* December 1996, p. 3.
2. For specific guidelines on having a personal retreat, see "The Process of Soul Sweating" in my book *Fatal Illusions: Shredding a Dozen Unrealities That Can Keep Your Organization From Success* (New York: AMACOM, 1997), pp. 200–202.
3. Robert L. Dilenschneider, *On Power* (New York: HarperCollins, 1994), p. 100.
4. M. Scott Peck, *People of the Lie* (New York: Touchstone Books, 1983), p. 218.

10

Conquering the Factors That Breed Independence

The purpose of freedom is to create it for others.
—Bernard Malamud

In the life of nations, especially in times of turmoil, they call them "rebel factions."

Individuals and teams doing "their own thing," when the "thing" isn't aligned with organizational visions or goals, is not a pretty sight.

The part that is really interesting, and also really frustrating, is that independence is always a possibility when a group of people gather together. But in general, counterproductive independence won't flourish unless it has fertile ground in which to grow.

It's our job as leaders to ensure that such fertile soil never becomes available. This isn't as hard as it sounds, because we're the ones who usually provide the ground.

Thinking that "there's no destructive, independent activity going on in our organization" would be, for most of us, a frightful illusion. To illude that everyone is moving together at all times isn't reality and isn't healthy. We're able to wallow in this illusion because the independent efforts are often disguised.

The disguise can take various forms, such as:

• *Changing the language, so that independent efforts are described as their opposites.* For instance, "we ended our alliance with that supplier for the good of the organization, since the supplier was confused about our internal cohesiveness and kept violating our chain of command."

• *Conducting guerrilla warfare.* In this case, land mines are planted throughout the organization and are found only after someone is wounded or killed (discredited or terminated).

• *Simply keeping activities secret.* An example of this is the salesperson who delays or alters paperwork in order to conceal the fact that he or she has extended credit to an unapproved customer.

The Factors That Breed Independence in Individuals

If we want to rid our organizations of collaboration-slaughtering independence in individuals, we've got to eliminate the factors that breed it. These include the following.

Punishment for Telling the Truth

Truth telling is a community enterprise.

Finding, knowing, and believing the truth comes from individual soul sweat. Others can point the way, but ultimately we have to do the work alone. But telling the truth is a social event. This is true for several reasons: There are others who need or deserve to hear the truth; telling it builds relational trust and the social fabric; and not telling it, whether by keeping silent or by lying, is a betrayal of a relationship and a tearing of the social fabric.

When people are punished for telling the truth, the authority doing the punishing is saying that it doesn't believe in true community. Interdependence can be built only on truth and trust. Saying "We don't want to hear the truth that you possess" has an echo: "You'll have to go your own way."

Suggested Solution: We have to do the obvious but difficult thing: not punish people when they admit mistakes, express doubts about ideas or products or services, challenge the validity of "corporate wisdom," or point out fatal organizational illusions. But we have to do more. We have to create a culture in which truth telling is the norm. We have to recognize and reward truth telling. We have to show its positive effects (through such things as organizational stories and anecdotes) on others and the whole organization. And we have to insist that our people listen to uncomfortable truths with patience and humility rather than falling back on quick, arrogant, or nasty defenses.

"The first responsibility of a leader is to define reality," writes Max DePree.[1] That definition begins with a commitment to truth.

Lack of Clear Vision and Goals

If our people don't know where we're going, they aren't going to join us.

Powersharing with people when we don't have a clear vision and goals is a guaranteed producer of independence—probably very strong independence. They're going to have to make up their own visions and goals, which are unlikely to match ours, and then if we powershare with them they have the power to make theirs happen.

Lack of vision and goals combined with a lack of powersharing yields a dependent organization that's going nowhere, and will probably get there fast. Lack of vision combined with powersharing yields an independent organization that's going a lot of different places, and may get to all of them right before the organization dies.

Suggested Solution: We should never powershare with people until our vision and goals are clearly in place. And we need to make sure that the vision and goals are interdependent, things that have been mutually hammered out and agreed to, things that have mutual benefit for us and them.

Constantly Changing Priorities

When people don't know what's important because what's "important" keeps changing, they're destined to go their own way.

Even if we do have a vision in place, there are a large number of ways to achieve that vision. The best of those ways should rise to the top via the process of setting priorities. When this isn't done, people will fill in the blanks.

Change is a reality. The rapidly increased rate of change is also a reality. But in the midst of this reality, true leaders use their power constructively to establish priorities that have some longevity. They know that people can't hit a constantly moving target.

Suggested Solution: We have to take a lot of time before we establish organizationwide priorities. We have to take even longer before we adopt new leadership concepts or introduce major change initiatives, such as values-based management, business process reengineering, total quality management, or quality function deployment. We need to proceed cautiously because we know that clearly defined and articulated priorities are natural builders of interdependence. We also must make sure that our power isn't spread too thin, by keeping the number of these priorities small and their organizational appeal wide.

Irregular or Absent System of Accountability

Without accountability, we'll get independence whether or not we powershare with our people. With powersharing thrown in, we just get it good and hard.

From the recovering alcoholic who has an accountability partner to the president of the United States who has a constitutional and legislative check and balance, from a feedback system to a board of directors, accountability is crucial to the construction of interdependence. This is so that people will be held accountable for meeting the priorities, achieving the goals, and keeping the commitments that have been mutually agreed upon as being critical and valuable contributions to the organization's success.

While there is truth in the old statement that "character is what you do in the dark," it's also true that character is what you do in the light (and how you respond when what you do in the dark comes to light).

Suggested Solution: We must have a system of accountability whose primary purpose is the achieving of important results and the building of interdependence rather than controlling people's thoughts and actions. Accountability often means "We're going to check up on you to see if you're doing it our way." But true, and effective, accountability focuses on results rather than methods, on performance rather than behavior (so some "unique" behavior is okay and not interpreted as "independence"), on the impact on synergy rather than the impact on organizational "norms."

Accountability can be a marvelous tool for enhancing individual potential and gluing an organization together through the expected enforcement of commitments and promises.

For meddlers, though, it can be a tool for intruding and annoying and confusing. For controllers, it can be an instrument of manipulation and rigidity and coercion. And for tyrants, it can be a tool of the devil.

Overfocus on Individual Performance and Incentives

Somehow, we continue to focus on individuals with our performance evaluations and incentive plans and still expect to get top-notch collaboration. Illusion lives on.

We focus on the individual partly because of history and inertia. Performance evaluations have always been applied to individuals. We've always done it that way. But we also focus on individuals because it's really hard to evaluate and reward teams and other collaborative efforts. Group projects come and go, some of them very quickly. And everyone involved in the effort doesn't contribute equally. So what should we do? Evaluate and reward everyone the same? Or vary our ratings on the basis of the individual's contribution to the group's effort?

Suggested Solution: The answer is not just to reward collaboration, because we do also need individual initiative. But most organizations are woefully weak on effectively rewarding and recognizing collaboration. We need to tackle the painstaking task of constructing an evaluation/reward system that gives equal weight to individual and collaborative efforts. And—here's a key—part of the evaluation of individual effort must be related to how that effort contributed to the community, and part of the response to collaborative effort needs to be related to how that effort improved the performance and potential of individuals elsewhere in the organization.

We need to build in incentives like team productivity bonuses, rewards based on the number of new ideas generated and/or implemented by a team, and pay-for-results plans.

Lastly, we need to have incentives for individual performance that don't encourage dog-eat-dog competition within the organization. To have those kinds of incentives while preaching collaboration is akin to handing children guns and exhorting them not to pull the trigger.

Ruthless competition should be severely limited to the motto of the Apollo 13 engineers: "Ruthlessly compete against your own best self."

Instability: Mobility, Transfer, and Turnover

Unstable environments always produce independence.

"Everyone did as he saw fit," an old writer said in describing a time of great instability.

Much of modern life has become essentially nomadic, involving moves from city to city, job to job, friend to friend. Whereas people used to think more in terms of community, now the focus is on self, because self is the only constant in a swirling existence. For many, the nuclear family is the last remaining fragment of community. (Is it called "nuclear" because it's built around a nucleus, or because it's about to blow up?)

Much of the advice given to individuals and organizations seems not only to approve of this transience but to encourage it. We're told to plan on having three careers and ten or more job changes before we retire. Leaders are advised to tell their people that we can't guarantee anything except that we'll help you with your "employability" (that is, elsewhere). We're told to move people around a lot to different jobs and different locations, which can be valuable advice up to a point (so long as it increases perspective and develops skills), but at a certain level keeps people superficial and disconnected both from people *and* from the results of their decisions. We're encouraged to believe that turnover is a good thing (even though, if we don't have an interdependent organization, the best people are often the ones who leave while the deadbeats stay on and on).

We can't have interdependence if we can't depend on each other being there tomorrow. Soldiers who see a series of buddies killed often learn the cruel lesson that they can't depend on anyone but themselves.

Suggested Solution: As leaders, we've got to slow down the pace of people-movement so that we can handle the increase in the pace of marketplace change. If both are changing fast, there are too many uncontrolled variables in the equation. We need to let people work together long enough so that they develop an intuitive understanding, an ease of collaboration, an unspoken connectedness. To be sure, this connectedness has to be balanced against the benefits of job rotation and fresh challenges, but a lot of this cross-training and personal development can occur within groups or teams. Even as we assign people in different combinations, we should always be alert to the advantages of bringing successful teams (as measured by results) back together to handle a new crisis or opportunity.

We should minimize turnover (and it's ugly twin, bulimic downsizing) by careful additions and selections of the right people. Corporate terminations (and the stench of death that accompanies them) can produce the same effect on collaboration and community that the "black death" had on people in the fourteenth century, when "a third of the world died" (a percentage equivalent to that in many organizational downsizings): "Nobody wept no matter what his loss," writes Barbara Tuchman, "because almost everyone expected death. . . . [It] was not the kind of calamity that inspired mutual help. . . . Behavior grew more reckless and callous, as it often does after a period of violence and suffering."[2] Powersharing and collaboration in the wake of massive instability in the community is pure illusion.

Difficulty in Obtaining Support or Permission

Even those who want to work cooperatively will finally give up in frustration if they can never get the support or permission of authority. Whether it's because of stuck-in-the-mud thinking from above or ten levels of required approvals, some people are just going to go their own way.

"It's easier to ask forgiveness than permission" is both a truism and a shame. In so many organizations, the only way to get something done is just to do it. Fear can work to inhibit this often healthy response, but the "underground market" in unapproved activity will continue. It can be driven into the shadows, but it is very hard to kill. It's easier to turn it by pressure into antiorganizational behavior.

Requirements for hierarchical support and approval create an environment in which those at the top of the hierarchy can exercise "leadership by veto." It's always easier to be an outsider and boo or dissent than it is to offer a constructive program of your own. Is it any wonder that people will just stop asking? Or, at the worst, doing?

Suggested Solution: The most important thing we can do is powershare with people to a level where support (from above, below, and all around) is easy to garner if the idea is good, and required permissions from anywhere are few and far between. In fact, we need to drive the whole concept of "permission" (and its co-controller, "approval") out of our thinking, with all its connotations of servitude and the parent-child relationship. In a free society, we don't have to get approval to go where we want to on vacation, or get permission to buy a house. Somehow, by and large, things still work. A free society—now *that's* a definition of maximum initiative *and* collaboration.

Carelessness in Hiring

Some people aren't going to cooperate no matter what. And others will do so only in certain situations.

Discerning the difference between initiative and independence isn't easy, but it's a must if we're going to build a functioning, interdependent society in our organization. In fact, many people are themselves unclear about the difference. Some think they were showing initiative in a previous job, when they were really working contrary to the organization's vision or priorities. Others are afraid they were being independent (and might even have been fired because of it) when they simply violated a mindless or counterproductive company rule.

Suggested Solution: Take a lot of time in hiring. Run people through multiple personality tests and avoid the people who score "Napoleon" (we also, of course, should avoid those who score "Walter Mitty"). Put people in simulations, real organizational situations that call for an interdependent response, and note *in detail* how they react. Have interviewees elaborate on both their individual and collaborative efforts, asking them which they liked best and why, asking them for examples of effective teamwork, their analysis of problems with past team efforts, their descriptions of what they think an effective team looks like, and instances of their own team leadership.

Insufficient or Absent Training in Teamwork

Lock them in a room and watch the teamwork grow.

Watch the bodies pile up, more likely.

Teamwork never just "happens." Sometimes, it doesn't happen even when we've done a lot of work to *make* it happen. Working together with other people is incredibly annoying unless we know how to do it.

Suggested Solution: We have to give people extensive training in teamwork, which includes reading (yes, we can require people to read), listening to tapes, attending seminars, participating in simulations, and responding to "what if" scenarios. Then we have to test the results of the training to see if they got it. Listen in (as in "attending but not talking") on team meetings and see if you can hear the faint sounds of interdependence.

Inconsistent or Confusing Communication

When people don't know what's going on, they do one of the most independent things human beings can do: They make it up.

They fill in the gaps, usually, with rumors, faulty information, propaganda, and guesses. People always work to construct a whole picture of reality in their minds, and without our help the picture can be a real work of fiction worthy of Hemingway.

Poor or absent communication is perhaps the biggest time

waster in organizations, and that's its *best* point. Much worse is its effect on people's attitudes, as they learn to live by guesses and assumptions.

Suggested Solution: Communicate *consistently,* meaning you should pick a few important topics and stay with them for a long time. No "idea of the month" or so much information that nobody can digest it all. Articulate the points you have selected in a variety of ways—by stories and anecdotes, by proper reinforcement—so people will really believe that these are the issues that are truly important to the organization. We need to really "open up the books" on those issues. "Open-book management is a process. You have to open up communication for it to be effective."[3]

Finally, we have to give the communication "closure." We have to get feedback. We have to know what they think we're saying. We have to learn what they need to hear that we're *not* currently saying. We have to find out what we are saying that they think is nonsense. In short, we have to have conversation, not just communication.

The Factors That Breed Independence in Teams

Teams started with Adam and Eve. And there's been glory and disaster in teamwork ever since.

Teams can take many forms—work teams, project teams, product development teams, problem-solving teams, cross-functional teams. Teams can produce outstanding results, far beyond what an individual can do in both breadth and depth. Ideas and solutions can develop at breakneck speed as the fire from one team member becomes the fuel for another.

But powersharing with a group, a team, can be even scarier than powersharing with an individual. There are more people, and more ways, to abuse the power. It's a lot harder to control a group of people and the wild synergy that can result from their efforts than it is to control just one person. That's one reason people who like to be in control can become *really* paranoid about teams.

Whole revolutions have started as the result of a powerful

team coming together. Some of these have been nonviolent, like the Constitutional Convention that was supposed to revise the Articles of Confederation in 1787 but instead used its power to create a whole new constitution for the United States of America; in fact, its members literally created the United States as we know it. And some of these powerful teams have produced violent revolutions, like the accepted and elected Nazi party that tore not only Germany but most of Europe to shreds.

Once we release power by powersharing with teams, there's no way to predict or control the outcome. And this is why it's so easy not to create teams at all or, if we do, to disempower them when they start getting "too big for their britches" (forgetting that a growing entity will *always* get too big for its britches).

The good news is that powersharing with teams doesn't have to lead to independent action. We can stop any counterproductive independence in its tracks.

We can't stop it with heavy-handed orders and proclamations: "Henceforth, all teams in this organization will exhibit no independence from the organization, under penalty of the guillotine." Our order won't work to end the independence; it will instead probably work to increase it, at least in subtly expressed and underground ways, and will divert our time and energy from important leadership activities and lead us to frustration.

But we can reduce the likelihood of independent activity if we minimize or eliminate the factors that can produce counterproductive independence in our projects, departments, and divisions.

Absence of a Coordinating Vision

Interdependent teams have to have a coordinating vision.

No team will be willing to sacrifice its time or resources to another team if it can't see how doing so will help the whole.

This narrow view of life and purpose can be compounded by a common organizational learning disability: We may think that we have a unifying vision because we've printed a statement on paper or on a plaque on the wall, when the truth is that vision statements have value only when they come to life in the words and actions of leaders. Only leaders can make a coordinating vision a daily reality. All leaders have to be "visionary" in the sense of embodying the organizational vision. And there *must* be leaders, even in "self-managed" and "self-directed" teams. In fact, especially there.

Suggested Solution: Leaders have to be the "point" people, like the person out in front of his platoon on patrol. Leaders are point people by living out in the future, walking ahead of our teams, finding the land mines and snipers, securing a safe place to bivouac for a bit before regrouping and moving on.

We have to have a vision, meaningful to everyone, or at least nearly everyone, in the organization, and detailed enough to give real direction to daily team activity.[4] We need to show our team leaders how they can actually gain power by concretizing the future, which will increase the power and effectiveness of the team. And we have to ensure that those leaders embody the vision of our organization and have the ability to convey it often and well to the team and to other leaders.

By *embody* I mean that they don't just understand the organization's vision intellectually but rather that they absorb it, have a sense of its nuances, a feel for it emotionally, an idea of what it means and doesn't mean, an appreciation of its values, an *investment* in it because it is theirs. We don't want people to be brainwashed or propagandized into agreeing with something that is in fundamental opposition to their core beliefs and values; rather, we want people whose core beliefs and values align with our organization's.

Finally, these leaders themselves must be authorized to redirect team activity when it moves in an independent direction.

Values Not Shared by All Team Members

If people don't share some basic values with those on their team and with the organization at large, misdirection and independence are a certainty.

The real problem often lies in the initial selection and assignment of people. Too many organizations haven't clearly defined and articulated their values, and even if they have they often don't bring these values up for response by the prospective employee in an interview. How can we expect commitment and dedication from people who intrinsically don't care about our values? Are we willing to be fooled by the ability of some people to discern what our values are and pretend that they share them?

The same principle applies to the selection and assignment of people to teams. Team leaders have to be "carriers" of the organization's values. And a team has to have at least a sizable minority of people who believe in our values completely.

Getting people who understand and agree with our values is complicated today by the explosion of knowledge and the resultant specialization of education and careers. People come to collaborative efforts with a perspective that is both unique and extremely narrow. It is clear today that no one can be a true "Renaissance" person in the sense of being intimately acquainted with the breadth of human knowledge. It is equally clear that we need to have people who are willing to see more than their own little world can show them.

Suggested Solution: The two great pieces of information to learn when hiring people are their interests and values, *not* their education, experience, and credentials. Their interests will determine their long-term satisfaction and effectiveness. Their values will determine whether they strengthen or diminish the organization's culture, and whether they move with or against our deepest convictions. Almost anything can be learned by people who are interested in a particular subject and believe it to be important, regardless of their credentials.

Once people are on board, we've got to ensure that we put only those people in team leadership positions who have been deeply immersed in, and reflexively believe in, the organization's values. We should work to build teams that always have at least a few members who *passionately* believe in our values. They'll never be quiet about behavior that is independent of those values.

Finally, we need to require our people to do two things that might seen self-contradicting but are actually unifying at the deepest levels: First, they need to become even more adept in their specialty field of knowledge; second, they need to continually work to broaden their worldview. To help them, we should put people into uncomfortable assignments, mix them with people from wildly different backgrounds, and require a certain amount of learning outside their specialty—from seminars, books, and tapes. I, for example, wouldn't have a scientist or engineer working for me who hadn't read a novel in years, or an advertising specialist who hadn't done some study in electronics or biology.

More specialty knowledge. And more knowledge about the world of which that specialty is just a tiny part.

Goals Unintegrated With Those of Other Teams

Few organizations have systems in place to ensure cross-collaboration among teams.

The result? Multiple teams making the same mistakes. Resources wasted reinventing wheels that are already spinning nearby. Advances by one team not shared with others. And a culture of independence.

Suggested Solution: We need to develop a culture in which teams are required to keep each other posted and have a simple way to get it done. One approach is through a weekly or biweekly report in a very simple and abbreviated one-page form that includes a number of headings:

- Statement of current and long-term goals
- Summary of progress made since last report
- Insights and possible insights made
- Description of obstacles encountered and solutions for overcoming them
- Warnings about pitfalls
- Requests for help or ideas

The purpose of this report is to share information, not to create a monitoring system. "Open-book management" isn't just from leadership to the rest of the organization; it has to include the pieces of the organization with each other. Our role as leaders isn't to query teams, collect the information, and carry it to everyone we can think of who needs it. Our role is to lead the creation, nurturing, maintenance, and streamlining of the system—the network—that will enable others to do it for themselves.

We can't assume that it will just "happen," because it won't.

Lack of Incentives to Share, and of Penalties for Not Sharing, Knowledge

We can assume that people will share what they know and learn.

We'll probably be disappointed.

Even the reporting just suggested won't be enough to get all the "tacit knowledge" that is embedded in our organizations out on the table where it can be seen and used. In a busy life, people's natural resistance both to telling potential internal "competitors" what they know and to taking the time to do it will keep them from talking unless there are some strong and compelling reasons to do so. So teams will simply go their own way and hoard their knowledge as a hedge against disempowerment.

Leverage is the key and the goal. How do we make transparent, and find ways to utilize, every drop of knowledge that we possess?

Suggested Solution: We must create incentives to share. These can include rewards to the teams that share the greatest number of ideas, or account for the greatest number of ideas utilized or implemented by other teams. Rewards can include team bonuses or increased budgets and responsibility. Penalties for not sharing can include reduction in bonuses and decreased budgets and responsibility (How can we justify giving you these things if you hoard, rather than multiply, the results?).

As with individuals, we can have our teams keep a log of innovations large and small, of mistakes made and corrected, and of obstacles overcome. One column on each of these logs should be headed "others with whom we have shared this knowledge."

How will we know if they didn't share? We may not, but only if they choose not to give themselves credit. And what if they don't have any good ideas?

Hasta la vista, team.

Absence of Incentives for Cooperation

This point is similar to the previous one, but here we're focusing on collaborative efforts rather than on the sharing of knowledge.

Fluidity is the key to success. Whether we talk in terms of "agile," "lean," or "adaptable," what we mean is something that has a flexible rather than a rigid structure. Firmly set and largely immovable departmental boundaries, and functional (rather than work-cell) manufacturing layouts, have the same saving value as the Maginot Line did for the French in 1940—zero.

There are so many disincentives to cooperation—the time it takes, the barriers we can erect to "just doing it"—that we will have to plot very thoroughly to come up with a plan that will surmount the hurdles.

Suggested Solution: We can survey teams to find out which ones have helped others the most often and the most effectively. We can evaluate which teams most often draw on the active involvement of others and suggest joint ventures. Some of these incentives can go to the individual team members who are most oriented toward active collaboration with other people and teams. One of the important ties between individual and team incentives is to reward *individuals* in part for their support of *teams.*

We also need to move people around periodically so that they can't build a power base and have to take a broader perspective. We can reward them for the prior experience that they integrate (not dump) into the new team. We have to find new and creative ways to build intraorganizational flexibility and cooperation into the culture.

One of the issues organizations have to face, for example, is whether to centralize or decentralize support services. Those favoring centralization argue for its economy of scale, elimination of duplication, and prevention of independence run amok. Those for decentralization argue for its accessibility by individual business units and its flexibility in meeting the needs of its customers. Some thinkers are now presenting a third alternative, "shared services," in which the support services are organized into a separate business unit and treated as a third-party "internal outsource." The problem is that it is still a single, centralized operation. Sooner or later, people are going to find ways around using it, edicts requiring its use will be issued, and a de facto centralized bureaucracy will once again live and dominate.

The answer is to allow each business unit to develop its own

support services, and for those service groups to be allowed—
and where appropriate, *required*—to "sell" their services internally to other business units. Then we can let the internal free
market do the necessary "centralizing." Instead of ten support
service groups, or just one, we'll probably end up with two or
three major "suppliers" and a few "specialty" or "niche" provid-
ers. The result? True collaboration, with independence limited
by market forces rather than by smothering and often ineffective
edicts.[5]

Poor Blending of Personalities

If team members don't connect with each other, the inevitable
results are antagonism, backbiting, the emergence of cliques,
and portions of the team and the team itself operating indepen-
dently.

With so many tools available to determine personality orientation and interests, it is amazing that so few of them are actually
used in forming teams. The usual first priority is to get a blending
of skills or people from different disciplines. This approach will
only accidentally build a team capable of exceeding the sum of
its parts.

Suggested Solution: I've emphasized several times the importance of selecting the right people for assignments and of
matching them with other people in a way that will produce synergy rather than holocaust. Teams need a balance of personalities, both to produce a melting pot of ideas and a system of
checks and balances within the team.

If a team has quality members and good training but still
doesn't jell, it doesn't mean that powersharing and teams don't
work. It simply means that *this* team doesn't work. The missing
ingredient is chemistry. Accept it and rearrange the teams.

Focus on Internal Rather Than External Drivers

No organization can look first for cohesiveness to its internal
drivers—politics, systems, structure, processes, culture—and
hope to avoid the push for independence in its teams.

It's the looking *outside* that forces us to unify around a common purpose or to stand against a common enemy. Many nations have been torn by factions and squabbling right up to the onset of a depression or an invasion by a foreign army. The question isn't "What are we doing?" but rather "What do they want us to be doing?"

Suggested Solution: We need to focus relentlessly on results and customer needs rather than on methods and organizational needs. We need to emphasize to our people that the organization exists to serve a higher purpose, not just to give us a place to go every day and fight for our piece of the pie. We must try to tap into people's need to make a difference and to leave a legacy. And we need to reward and recognize those who are constantly talking about "our *customers'* needs" rather than "our needs."

Unchanneled or Uncontrolled Passion

Passion is indispensable for long-term success. Nothing will substitute for it.

But passion let loose can lead in a thousand independent directions. Within the confines of our R&D department (and we should have one of these, even if we're in the service business), a lot of independent directions might be acceptable, even good, but in the organization at large it's a formula for self-induced chaos.

Suggested Solution: We need to give people a high enough vision and lofty enough goals to bring out their best passion, then give them a forum for using it. We need to find out what people are passionate about and work hard to let them do it— and we shouldn't have any people who aren't passionate about *something.*

The key here is *balance.* We don't just want to have a few major thrusts at any point in time; none of them may grab the passions of many of our people, none of them may represent our real future no matter how passionate some people are about them. But too many possibilities leave us unfocused, and even a vast quantity of passion can seep away without impact. There is no fixed number, but the thrusts that exist should be fixed in the minds of a number of passionate people.

Overuse of Rules

A philosopher by the name of Saul of Tarsus once asked, "Why . . . do you submit to [other people's] rules: Don't handle, don't taste, don't touch? These are all destined to perish. . . . These kinds of regulations do indeed appear to be wise . . . but they have no restraining value."

Excessive rules are almost guaranteed to bring about the opposite of what we want: They trigger something in human nature that makes us want to break them. Some people may not do so, out of fear of the consequences or because of the way they were raised, but many people will be tempted to break at least the most annoying rules.

In too many organizations, people are choked with rules. Proliferation of rules is a sure sign of the fossilization of the organization and of its loss of soul. At some point, the whole concept of rules becomes meaningless, as their number multiplies and new ones have to be issued to interpret and deal with violations of loopholes in the existing rules. "Great groups tend to be nonconformist. People in them are always rule busters. . . . People in great groups are always on their own track."[6]

Suggested Solution: Have the fewest possible number of rules: One is better than two, two are better than three. We need to remember the wisdom of James Madison in *The Federalist:*

> It will be of little avail to the people that the laws are made by men of their own choice, if the laws be so voluminous that they cannot be read, or so incoherent that they cannot be understood; if they . . . undergo such incessant changes that no man who knows what the law is today can guess what it will be tomorrow. Law is defined to be a rule of action; but how can that be a rule, which is little known, and less fixed?[7]

We need to focus on vision and values and getting the right people involved, and bury the impulse to make rules.

I want people working for me who remember Henry David Thoreau's "rule": "Any fool can make a rule, and every fool will mind it." Pity the organization that isn't made up of people who will break the rules to achieve the goals.

Hypocrisy in Organizational Leadership

If we in positions of formal authority say one thing and do another, people will feel free to make up their own idea of leadership. And, in the gaps, they'll feel free to do whatever they want.

One hypocrisy is to pretend that leadership has been transferred to the team when in reality it still resides at the top of the organizational hierarchy. This often occurs where those in authority believe that power really is a limited commodity and that a sharing of power means a loss of power. A second hypocrisy is to pretend that the team has power when in reality it can do nothing without "clearance."

Suggested Solution: We have to accept—by faith, if necessary—that power really does multiply when it is shared or given away. "Power need not be a zero-sum proposition. . . . The more power and influence a leader has, the better off the team will be."[8] We need to pour power into team leadership and the teams themselves—or, rather, draw out the power that already exists. And we have to maximize the number of decisions a team can make, including spending decisions, without any additional approvals.

●

Passionate, vision-believing, values-sharing, collaborative, well-designed, properly focused, rule-ignoring individuals and teams are the most effective and dynamic route to ongoing and sustainable success. Interdependent people who value the performance of everyone else. Free to go their own way, as long as it's in the same general direction.

The goal is to have people who know when to take charge and when to kick a decision up the line, how to communicate with those around them and those in formal authority, and what they should do alone and what they need help to accomplish.

The quality and sincerity of what we say is one critical element of interdependence. "Some companies," Jim Harris writes, "change the words they use to describe each other in the hope of creating a stronger sense of internal partnership . . . but just changing a few words without embracing the core strategies that actually create vibrant partnerships only creates a partnership facade.'"[9] We have to say the words, even change the words, but the words have to reflect who we really are and what we really intend to do.

●

Finding the balance.

That's what we've been trying to do in this section of the book. Dependence and independence are unhealthy extremes that will take a toll on our competitive position. And the tragedy is, we'll be doing it to ourselves.

By attacking the extremes, the flanks, we can force the action to the center.

Interdependence.

Notes

1. Max DePree, *Leadership Is an Art* (New York: Bantam Doubleday Dell, 1989), p. 11.
2. Barbara W. Tuchman, *A Distant Mirror* (New York: Ballantine Books, 1978), pp. 95, 96, 117.
3. Leslie Fishbein, as quoted in "Why Open The Books," *Inc.,* November 1996, p. 95.
4. For a detailed discussion of vision statements, real and illusory, see Chapter 4 in my book *Fatal Illusions: Shredding a Dozen Unrealities That Can Keep Your Organization From Success* (New York: AMACOM, 1997).
5. For a full and excellent treatment of this concept, see Gifford and Elizabeth Pinchot, *The Intelligent Organization* (San Francisco: Berrett-Koehler Publishers, 1996).
6. Warren Bennis and Patricia Ward Biederman, "The Secrets of Creative Collaboration," *Inc.,* December 1996, p. 98.
7. *The Federalist,* Jacob E. Cooke, ed. (Middletown, Conn.: Wesleyan University Press, 1961), p. 421.
8. J. M. Wilson, J. George, R. S. Wellins, and W. C. Byham, *Leadership Trapeze: Strategies for Leadership in Team-Based Organizations* (San Francisco: Jossey-Bass, 1994), p. 8.
9. Jim Harris, "The Partnership Facade," *Management Review,* April 1996, p. 45.

The Quality of Power

11

Constructive Power

Character is power.
—Booker T. Washington,
Black American educator
and leader

All eyes turned toward Wess.

Somehow, in a way no one could explain later, the decision about the major product revision fell to Wess.

He hadn't said much at any of the fourteen previous meetings. He had submitted no documents. He had neither agreed nor disagreed with any of the four strong positions still in the running. And his title—product development specialist—paled beside those of most of the people who were now looking at him so expectantly.

Wess had grabbed everyone's attention with a simple comment offered in the midst of a furious exchange between the vice president of marketing and the operations manager. He had said, simply, "I have a summary here that might point the way to the answer."

In the seconds that followed, even before anyone had seen Wess's summary, an unspoken consensus formed that his conclusions should be implemented—whatever they were.

The Nature of Constructive Power

Constructive power is a compelling force that derives its effectiveness from truth and wisdom. It uses vision, shared beliefs, persuasive gifts, expertise, reason, and example to motivate others. Because it's based on principles rather than externalities, its application results in multiplied organizational power and influence.

Constructive power is based on truth. Truth can free organizations to change, to grow, to strengthen themselves. Wisdom—the proper understanding and application of truth—can take our power to the next level and make us a success in every sense of the word. "Wisdom makes one wise person more powerful than ten rulers in a city," says an old proverb. Power based on anything but truth and wisdom will be ineffective or destructive.

Great damage can be caused by having too little constructive power or by having it in too few hands.

What was the basis of Wess's stunning power, power that far exceeded his position or title? His power derived from the respect others had for his truthfulness and wisdom.

As for his truthfulness, he had come to be known as a person without political ambition or any axes to grind. He said what was on his mind, but always briefly and graciously. He had a way of cutting through irrational arguments to get to the rational roots or, even more important, to the nonrational core of the problem. Uncannily, he always seemed to have at his fingertips the key fact or data that showed the way out of the dilemma.

Such a high percentage of his suggestions had turned out to be sound that his competence was respected even by those who disagreed with him on any given point. People believed him to be both impartial and sincere. "It was really frustrating at first," his boss would tell people from time to time. "Just when you'd think he was with you, he'd say something that would torpedo your position. Only after a while did you come to see that he wasn't with *you*—he was with the *truth*, wherever that seemed to take him. It made me mad—it still does at times. But it always makes me listen."

As for his wisdom, Wess was recognized as someone who was both keenly aware of the pressing nature of market forces and strongly resistant to hasty and ill-considered concepts. He tied his recommendations into both the organization's vision and the beliefs and goals of the key decision makers—whoever they were on a given issue. And regardless of whether the decision went his way or not, he went about the business of implementing it with both cheerfulness and humility.

He refused to be drawn into any long-term factions over short-term disagreements. And he often found a way to console and encourage those who had apparently "lost" on that decision. When someone would try to point out that a specific decision or direction was not the one Wess thought was best, his usual response was disarming: "I'd feel a lot worse about it if I were infallible. And I'd keep fighting if I thought this decision would break us, but I don't think it will. And, you know, when I consider how many lousy decisions I've made, it makes me give other people a lot of room."

The usual sources of power are considered to be position (power bestowed by ownership, organizational fiat, or fear), expertise (power acquired by education, training, experience, knowledge, or reasoning ability), charisma (power garnered by personal attraction, emotional appeal, compelling ideas, or persuasive ability), effort (power gathered by hard work and dedication), and relationship (power accumulated by networking, communication skills, integrity, and reputation).

All of these *are* sources of constructive power. Leaders who want to maximize their power will try to draw from as many of these sources as possible. But without truth and wisdom at the core, these means can also be sources of destructive power.

"The attempt to combine wisdom and power has only rarely been successful and then only for a short while," said physicist Albert Einstein. If that's so, then in organizations today we'd better learn how to do it better.

Building on Wisdom and Truth

Building on truth simply means correlating our mental models, ideas, and beliefs with reality. Given human nature and the complexity of the workplace and society, this is always an approximation. But it is very important that we make the best approximation possible at each point in time, and that we be constantly ready to modify our perspective as new information and knowledge demand a course correction.

It is incredible how tenaciously we can cling to outmoded, simplistic, erroneous, and even ridiculous ideas. Our own laziness and prejudices are compounded by the fact that most of what we "know" is from hearsay, inference, and assumption rather than from what we have actually witnessed or experienced. A lot of humility is needed here. Constructive power is seldom wielded by those who think they have a corner on the truth.

Wisdom is simply finding truth and using it in a constructive way. Wise power has seven pillars. It is:

1. *Other-centered.* Constructive power can't be wielded from an orientation of envy and personal ambition. Its starting point has to be the good of all the organization's stakeholders, and the conviction that this decision, act, or policy will, as a corollary, benefit me.

2. *Cooperative.* Constructive power generally has to be built on collaboration, consensus, and alliances rather than on a spirit of war-like competitiveness (internally or externally) that can lead to bitterness and resentment. Our real competition isn't even our fiercest external competitor; rather, it's a future marketplace reality that we must envision, customer needs that customers themselves haven't as yet articulated or even realized, out-of-sight organizations rearranging the very basis of competition, not-yet-imagined-or-invented products or services, and our own internal illusions and lunacies. We'll need the help of all our stakeholders to stand up to *this* competition. There's room to have healthy, free-market competition internally and externally without having it turn ugly. It's amazing how many people are still promoting Darwinian, eat-your-young internal competition, all the while ignoring one of the oldest truths: A house divided against itself will fall. Constructive power loves peace without sacrificing principle.

3. *Considerate.* Even though they might have a "right" to be fearsome and punitive, users of constructive power lay down that right. Constructive power is uplifting, dignifying, and beneficial to those whom it touches. It has a leniency about it, not abusing people for mistakes and imperfections. And it recog-

nizes that the ends don't justify the means. Even if a Machiavellian approach might work in a given situation, it is passed up. Constructive power works just as well or better—and it reduces the probability of planned coups and assassinations.

4. *Ready to yield.* Constructive power refuses to be obstinate. It is willing to recognize when others have a better plan and then get behind it. It is willing to submit to others even of lower rank and to follow when following is appropriate.

5. *Productive.* Constructive power is full of organizational healing and positive results. It puts its energies where they can do the most good at any point in time.

6. *Impartial.* Constructive power doesn't play politics, shows no favoritism, and avoids discriminating against others for any reason. It avoids factions and cliques like the plague. And it refuses to be boxed, categorized, or labeled.

7. *Sincere.* Constructive power is based on walking an honest talk. It discerns and avoids hypocrisy. People who utilize constructive power know that genuineness and authenticity are linchpins of their long-term success.

This kind of power leaves a legacy that's strong on the bottom line as well as on the people issues. It's the kind of power that we can feel good about using, and the kind that we should expect to be used by those who have power.

Retaining and Sharing Constructive Power

Constructive power can be retained or shared. If constructive power is retained when it should be shared, the positive results are limited. This is so for two reasons: First, the vision is too narrow—alone, we can't see all the ways in which we might use our constructive power; and second, there is too little of it—its scope is too limited—to account for any significant change. Good intentions, hopeful ideas, but small results.

If constructive power is shared when and where appropriate, the positive results can be maximized. The sharing has to be wisely done. All of the wielders (or at least most of them) have to agree on the purposes. The positive effects will be reduced if some are confused about the purposes of its use or are afraid to use the power.

In Chapter 13, I'll discuss in detail how to put power in the right hands, and what those hands should look like.

Constructive Power and the Legitimization of Authority

Legitimate authority uses power constructively. In fact, legitimate authority is power used for the benefit of others. (I am using the terms *legitimate* and *illegitimate* power in nonstandard ways. Although those terms are usually used to describe the process by which people come to possess power, I am including the way in which they use it.)

Legitimate authority is concerned both with the proper acquisition of power—getting it by proper means—and with the proper purpose of power—using it for good. As economic justice involves both how we get and how we use money, so authority involves both how we get and how we use power.

Power is illegitimate if it is gotten through improper means. Those means include lying, withholding information, gossip, slander, manipulation, and destroying others.

Position or title can grant us entry to authority, but only the proper and constructive use of the power that this authority brings can legitimize it. And only the proper use of this level of power can make way for greater levels of legitimate and useful power. Appeals to status almost always lose their impact over time.

Weak—and illegitimate—managers never seem able to grasp this concept. Their thinking seems to stop at "I'm the boss, so you have to do this." Although it has the ring of legitimacy, it's the ring of the "divine right of kings," an idea that led to great rebellions and the decapitation of kings.

Weak and illegitimate managers constantly refer to their title and position. They have to, because they have never legitimized and extended their authority by the proper and consistent use of this power (by *consistent* I mean not using it constructively on one issue and destructively on another). In fact, they may have damaged or destroyed—illegitimized—their power by using it improperly or inconsistently or both.

People with legitimate authority, people who have learned to control and use power effectively for the benefit of all stakeholders, seldom or never refer to their title or position. They don't have to. They're walking the talk, so they don't have to talk.

●

Constructive power can create organizations where none existed before, build cities, move rivers, and change the course of entire nations or civilizations. It can come in the form of an influential book, a movie, a memo, a speech, a decision, or a radical change in direction. At bottom, constructive power is the force that makes anything of value occur.

But it has an evil twin.

12

Destructive Power

Get rid of abusive managers, even if they're stars.

—Mort Meyerson, as quoted
in *Bottom Line Personal*,
1 October 1997, p. 13

"I think I've got enough support to kill that proposed new product line," Brad said, grinning.

"That's great," Caroline responded, scanning the menu.

Brad felt good. He decided what to have for lunch, then leaned back comfortably in his chair. Light streaming through the curved, greenhouse-like windows cast gently swaying shadows on the wicker table and its surroundings.

Caroline closed her menu and laid it aside. "Who's come on board?" she asked.

Brad leaned forward and began turning his water glass slowly between his palms. "Max told me he was with me this morning. I already had commitments from Clark and Gabrielle."

"Gabrielle?" asked Dale, who was still holding his menu in front of him.

"Yep."

Dale seemed very surprised. "Did she have any reservations?"

"No. Well, maybe a few."

"I really thought she was gung-ho on that new line," Caroline said.

"Me, too," Dale added.

Brad took a roll from the covered basket. "I think she was, at first. But when I kept pointing out the mixed results from our customer focus groups and the unresolved design issues, she didn't have anything to counter with." He began to butter the roll. "I also told her that if she helped me on this one, I'd help her push through that new distribution idea she's come up with."

"Brad, you're relentless," Caroline said approvingly, "This'll drive Wayne up the wall."

"I know it. He's been working on that thing for over two years."

"I'm not so sure this is right," Dale said softly.

Brad looked horrified. "What do you mean?"

"I just don't know," Dale said, finally closing his menu. "I'm just not sure killing that new line is the best thing for the company. I know there are some problems with market research and design, but I don't know if they're enough to kill it."

"I thought you hated Wayne," Brad said.

"I know you do," Caroline chimed in. "I remember how angry you were when he questioned your results on the Moran project in front of everybody."

"I was angry," Dale agreed. "I was mad enough to . . . anyway, I think he should have handled that differently. It was a meatball way to raise his objections. But that doesn't have anything to do with the viability of this new line."

"I'm really surprised," Brad said, disappointment filling his voice. "I thought you'd be with us."

"I just don't want to kill our future."

"To hell with that future," Brad retorted, his eyes flashing angrily. "That's Wayne's future, not ours."

The Evil Twin

Every good thing, like constructive power, has a shadow, an evil twin.

The roots of this pairing are found in our own human nature. We—at least most of us—have a side that wants to do good, wants to make a difference, wants to be respected, wants to be loved. But we have another side that's not so glorious. It's the side that wants to get even, wants to have its own way, wants to be in control, wants to be served. Those of us who want to live a significant, successful life (in all senses of these words) find ways to feed the "high" side and to starve the "low."

It does no good to pretend that there is no low side. Money, nice homes, expensive clothing, title, position, and fame won't make it go away. When we pretend it isn't there, we set ourselves up to be blindsided. We're left in shock that we could think, or say, or do such truly dreadful things.

It's comforting when we can come to the point of finally admitting it. People—including us—are *not* basically good. In fact, we can be a pretty miserable lot. And it's not just our environment that poisons us; if people are basically good, then where did the crummy environment come from in the first place? Look at the playground. Children say and do things to each other that adults, who understand the consequences of assault charges, seldom even consider. Look even earlier, at the nursery. Whom do babies care about? Us? No way. No one on earth is as self-centered as a baby. These little ones think only of themselves 90 percent of the time. The other 10 percent they're thinking of what we can do for them. The institution of slavery hasn't ended in the mind of a baby.

It's also illuding to think that these babies will outgrow their low sides. *We* haven't. That side is the shadow, always tracking closely behind us. We don't grow out of it, like we do baby teeth, bed-wetting, and acne.

The same is true in organizations. The shadow is always there, the coercive force that derives its effectiveness from status, such as position, credentials, fame, economic level, custom, public opinion, personal attractiveness, and physical strength. It uses secrecy, gossip, slander, fear, propaganda, symbols, and manipulation to control others. Because it's based on externalities and wrong motives, its application results in power centers, war zones, and shriveled organizational power and influence (because we believe that if we share power we'll have less of it for ourselves).

Too much of the writing and lecturing on powersharing (or "empowerment") is sheer fantasy. It presumes the existence of people whom none of us has ever met. It illudes that we can run an organization full of Pollyannas.

But all of us are flawed. Some of us are flawed really badly. Pretending the shadow doesn't exist sets us up as leaders to be taken by surprise when it is exercised. And our organizations won't grow out of it unless we can find a way to operate without any people. The Brads we will always have with us. Our job is to prevent as many of them as possible from getting in, and to prevent any that do make it in from staying in.

Clues to the Presence of Destructive Power

There are some criteria to determine if we are in the presence of destructive power. People who exercise it have these characteristics:

• *Desire for control.* For some people, the issue of control is uppermost in their minds. They are always talking about it, worrying about it, wanting it to be clarified. Life becomes a forum for dividing up and establishing control over others. This is driven by internal weakness. "The lust for power is not rooted in strength but in weakness," said psychoanalyst Erich Fromm.

• *Delight in failure.* Although most of us are pleased when something harmful to the organization is eliminated or a destructive person is terminated, that's not what we're talking about here. When a person delights in the failure of other people or their ideas, regardless of the value of those ideas or the heart that went into them, we should be extremely concerned. Envy can be just a frank recognition that someone has something *enviable* (that is, worth having). But the shadow side of envy goes beyond jealousy. This envy wants other people to fail. Jealousy wants what the other person has, while this envy, at the least, wants the other person not to have it.

• *Demand for recognition.* All of us want to be recognized for our talents and contributions. But when we sense that someone is pushing for recognition, we should pay closer attention. This disease often, if not always, has a corollary that begrudges recognition to others, whether they are subordinates or co-workers. Many people are like black holes, absorbing all recognition into the vast abyss within.

• *Self-righteousness.* We need to be able to distinguish this from cockiness. Cockiness, a frequent affliction of youth (although sometimes a chronic illness), is a self-assuredness that is usually unwarranted by the facts (such as talent, experience, wisdom). Self-righteousness is a smug certainty that we've got the answers, that most other people don't, and that the ones who don't are dirt. "They consider themselves super smart," writes Larry L. Axline, "but, in reality, they only talk more."[1] Cockiness has a way of being knocked out of us, starting on the playground. Self-righteousness, on the other hand, is harder to separate from a pompous person than money is from a politician.

• *Need to rationalize.* When people refuse to change their opinion or at least reconsider it in the face of massive evidence to the contrary, something unhealthy is going on. Although they can come up with elaborate rationalizations for why they are sticking to the absurd, these explanations are just a cover-up for the reality that they want things to be their own way, that they want the "reality" inside their own heads to count for more than the reality the rest of us are living in.

• *Use of flattery.* Destructive power seldom comes dressed in a red suit with horns and a pitchfork. It somehow knows that to accomplish its foul mission it has to cloak its intentions and its appearance. The most insidious of cloaks is one that goes the other way, that tells us we have a great idea while it is working behind the scenes to sabotage it. Flattery is a masquerade, but we'll have to get past our willingness to be taken in (because it feels so good to be told we're brilliant) to see that it isn't real—to see, in fact, that it's a Trojan horse.

• *Demoralization of others.* Morale is harder to measure than productivity, but that doesn't mean that it isn't measurable or worth measuring. Destructive power will take its toll on morale. We can look for the clues as we look at the results of each leader's performance: higher turnover, higher absenteeism, more tardiness, higher rate of injuries (particularly minor ones), and so forth. It's easy to label destructive power as being "tough" or "uncompromising," but we need to avoid this delusion.

Destructive Uses of Power

Since it comes from the shadowland, destructive power can be used for some purposes that the sane among us can't imagine, don't even want to imagine. Terminated workers come back to really terminate former bosses and fellow employees; people steal from the company and each other; people assault co-workers in the late-night parking lot; workplace violence has become page one news. Here, we won't be looking at destructive uses of power that take the form of criminal acts, but rather at those that can leave an organization in shambles and without legal recourse. These acts include:

• *Killing the future.* This is what Brad was doing in this chapter's opening story. New ideas are killed by the bucketful, not because they're bad or unprofitable but because they don't fit somebody's personal agenda for the future or because they're being championed by someone whom a destroyer hates. This use of destructive power *cannot be overestimated.*

• *Sidetracking careers.* Wielders of destructive power tend to view others as either allies or enemies (mostly enemies). They tend to focus on destroying specific individuals, particularly those who are successful, have the respect of others, and are effectively using constructive power. This is true partly because these people are in the way, partly because their agendas clash severely with that of the destroyer, and partly because the goal of destructive power is to tear down rather than to build up. We need to realize that our best people come with a built-in handicap—they have enemies who are sworn to destroying them.

• *Hindering the development of others.* In a less extreme expression of its malevolent nature, destructive power blocks the development of others and efforts to powershare with them because those are just nice "sensitivity" issues that have nothing to do with the bottom line. This approach is based on the idea that we will furnish the brains and they will furnish the backs, and is exemplified by the thought that "we're a no-nonsense bunch around here." It deliberately keeps people ignorant. "Knowledge is ruin to my young men," observed Adolf Hitler.

• *Demoralizing others.* This is the attitude of the "lean and mean" boss who knows how to "inspire" fear and trembling in the ranks. Instead of going after their paychecks and careers, however, the destroyer goes after their sense of worth and morale. This attitude is based on the idea that people are liabilities and cost drivers instead of assets and profit drivers, and is exemplified by the thought that "when we want your opinion, we'll beat it out of you." It comes in the form of belittling comments, criticism of all efforts, or public ridicule. It was the type of destructive power wielded by Wayne in the opening story, a type that invited a return of destructive power from others.

• *Playing favorites.* This form of destructive power is the opposite of sidetracking the careers of the destroyer's enemies. In this case, power is used to reward and advance the careers of those who kowtow to the destroyer. Its goal is to create a group of impotent followers. It leaves the organization with a circle of dependents, all of whom have the same dysfunctions as the wielder of power.

• *Majoring on the minor.* Destructive power moves our eyes away from the big picture, the prize, and onto the trivial. It recognizes that often the best way to destroy an organization is to get it looking through the wrong end of the telescope. Since it is small-minded, it also likes to focus on small things. Examples are the manager who wants to review every memo before it's sent; the owner who requires his signature on every requisition no matter how small; the supply clerk who locks up pencils; the accounting manager who reviews every code, keystroke, and print-out generated in her department. Its purpose is to make the wielder of power feel important by controlling other people. Getting others enmeshed in a never-ending review of policies or obsessed with a few people's "violations" of minor procedures is an excellent way to drain the life out of an organization.

• *Random actions or decisions.* In this case, power is used to make decisions not guided by the organization's vision and goals or even by any discernable logic. But there *is* an underlying rationale: The destroyer is "proving" that "I'm in charge and you have to do what I say." It also forces subordinates to take all decisions to the wielder of power because they can't possibly guess what the right answer is. Scott Adams, the creator of the cartoon strip "Dilbert," makes a living on this one.

• *Self-aggrandizement.* From the manager who requires his secretary to pick up his dry cleaning to the owner who cuts pay and benefits while using company funds to buy a condo at a resort, this is using power purely for the wielder's own benefit. It is based on the idea that "We've earned our position and they haven't," and is exemplified by the thought, "to the victor belong the spoils."

"There are two ways of exerting one's strength: one is pushing down, the other is pulling up," said Booker T. Washington. Wielders of destructive power always push down.

The Effects of Destructive Power

Like constructive power, destructive power also can be either retained or shared.

If destructive power is retained, negative results will be obvious. The results can be gigantic if the power holder is ruthless enough and the followers are sheep. The effects are often limited only by the level of control-freakishness and paranoia of the destroyer.

If the destructive power is shared, negative results can multiply dramatically. An old proverb says, "When the wicked rise to power, people go into hiding." When abusive power is unleashed in an organization, people have to find ways to "dodge the bullet." Much of the "CYA" behavior in organizations is built around the basic human difficulty of admitting mistakes (especially in an environment of fear), but a significant portion of it is also a defense against others using their power unjustly against us.

A distribution of power into abusive hands also "sells" everyone in the organization on the idea that this is what power is used for. When destructive power is the coin of the realm, people will feel forced to try to get some (through methods such as intimidation and slander) so they can "buy" what they need. It's very difficult to keep the use of power from degenerating everywhere when abusive power reaches a critical mass anywhere.

We shouldn't try to convince ourselves that this destructive power won't spill over into our dealings with our customers and other stakeholders. When people are treated abusively within an organization, whether by leaders or those to whom leaders have granted the exercise of power, it is impossible to expect them not to carry this abuse over into the outside world. A construction firm for which I was consulting once lost a major bid because its chief estimator addressed the project engineer in the same harsh, rude, and arrogant manner with which his boss frequently spoke to him.

As the contractor found out, destructive power will always bring about a reduction in power, either through the overt action of stakeholders or the covert action of peers and subordinates, who work to bring the power holder down.

Although destructive power is an ever-present dangerous reality and can't be exorcised, it can be recognized, minimized, and traumatized. As leaders of a small group or a giant enterprise, we can deal with it.

No fear.

Note

1. Larry L. Axline, "The Company Power Troll," *Management Review*, July–August 1997, p. 62.

13

One Side of the Balance: Putting Power Where It Needs to Be

Do we love others enough that if we had unwarranted
power over their lives, we would struggle to give it up?

—Richard Brookhiser,
Founding Father:
Rediscovering George
Washington, p. 193

We wouldn't give a loaded gun to a small child. We wouldn't give
the car keys to our ten-year-old. We wouldn't give our credit card
to a homeless person we've never met before with instructions
to "just use it for one meal and then return it."

Instinctively, we know that actions that in themselves might
be reasonable become very unreasonable when they involve people who aren't ready to participate at that level.

The same is true of power. It has force, like a gun, to stop
wrong actions. It has capability, like a car, to get us somewhere.
And it has usefulness, like a credit card, to get things done
quickly and efficiently. Or, in the wrong hands, it can get us
killed, sued, or bankrupted.

Who ought to have power? More specifically, who ought to
have the power that we are willing to share? In this chapter, we'll
take a look at the kinds of people who warrant receiving or getting to use additional power. In the next chapter, we'll analyze

the kinds of people who will abuse the power—and the organization, and us.

Critical Traits of the Power-Worthy

There are a number of important criteria that identify the people who are truly ready to wield more power. The ones who receive it should have:

An Acceptance of Power's Limitations

Power is most safely entrusted to people who know its limitations. These people know that power is only one of the tools available to solve a problem. And usually only part of the answer.

It is a deadly deception to believe that "If I just had more power, then I could. . . ." The idea of power as a cure-all is seductive but badly misleading.

People who know that they will still need help from above, below, and all around no matter how much power they are given are worthy receptacles of power. They're less likely to abuse power and waste power because they know that they'll have to rely on others in an interdependent reality to achieve success in the full meaning of that term. If they know that having power itself can be misleading (it can make us resort to power too soon) or unhelpful (it can keep us from looking at other resources or solutions), so much the better. Some national leaders have discovered this when they couldn't say "I'll have to check" in the middle of summit meetings or while they were personally handling negotiations.

Clues to a worthy person's character include: the absence of complaints about having too little power; a willingness to work through great challenges from a position of persuasiveness, influence, and negotiation rather than from a position or direct application of power; a penchant for seeking out and listening to widely divergent sources of counsel; and a delight in the discovery of talents and skills in the people around them. People who respond well to hardships, difficulties, and insults— meaning that they persist in trying to work through them while maintaining and quietly insisting on reasonable personal bound-aries—are also sending us the right signal, since they're showing that they understand that few things of value are accomplished easily or without opposition.

Watch for signs that people are cognizant of their own falli-bility. An open expression of doubt, a willingness to listen to others, and the use of consensus where appropriate are excellent clues. Deference to the wishes or concerns of others even when one strongly disagrees—so long as it isn't a matter of principle—can show an absence of cockiness and overconfidence. And look for someone who—for the right reasons, like refusing to com-promise and standing up for people—has walked away from power as embodied in position, title, pay, or benefits. These peo-ple respect power and are interested in using it for good, but know that power isn't to be had at any cost.

The norm is quite different. Power normally is pulled toward the already powerful, to those who are seeking power for themselves, to those who are sure that power is the "answer."

Flexibility

Prior to receiving an influx of new power or a release of the power that lies within them, people need to understand and ac-cept the fact that this allocation isn't a "once for all time" shar-ing, and that the level of power may go up or down over time as the needs of customers and the organization require. I'm not talking about giving and taking away promotions but rather about expecting everyone who works for us, whether they're in a formal position of authority or not, to know and accept that power is a *tool,* not a status symbol or birthright; that it isn't inherent in or permanently attached to a position; that power is something different from, and not coterminous with, position; and that our organization expects power to flow to where it is needed and can be used by the best-suited person, whether that person is the senior vice president or a frontline customer ser-vice representative (a.k.a. senior vice president of whether we stay in business over the long term).

Look for people who lay down power willingly and voluntar-ily, as George Washington and others did with the presidency of the United States, as the Emperor of Japan did with emperor worship in 1945, and as the British did with slavery in the nineteenth century. Pay attention to those who almost automatically begin sharing any newfound power with peers and subordinates. But make sure they share it *appropriately,* by which I mean the right amount with the right people, none with destructive people, and none that should be retained by them. Some people are like the basketball player who always passes and never shoots. Others collect power the way a black hole absorbs light—it all goes in, but nothing comes out.

Flexibility includes a capacity to deal with the ambiguous and undefinable. Much of what comes to us in life can't be sorted, classified, or quantified, at least not in the short run, and a lot of good power can be wasted trying to do these things. People who don't have to "do something" immediately in every situation, who are comfortable sitting still until a better moment arrives, are excellent repositories of power.

Graciousness

All of us have run into (or been run over by) mean people. Strong and nasty is a horrible combination, but strong and gracious can work well on all fronts.

People, egos, relationships, teams, and morale are all very fragile things. We need to give power to people who understand this and act on its implications. Among these implications is the concept that power should be used to protect rather than to dissect others. Another is that power *needs* to be used to forgive imperfections and mistakes. A third is that more power than we might generally realize should be used for healing—rather than shooting—the wounded.

This doesn't mean that people with power should shield others from reality or the consequences of their acts. It does mean that they should use power to drive fear out of the workplace by being and acting trustworthy, by avoiding overreaction, and by treating glitches with noninsulting humor. They should make room for the weaknesses, foibles, moods, and up-and-down swings that all of us are subject to. And they should understand the value of mistakes and not crucify either the one who made the mistake or the messenger who brought the bad news.

"Nothing is so strong as gentleness; nothing so gentle as real strength," said St. Francis de Sales.

Humility

God save us from the people who know everything and never make mistakes!

Power is well placed when it is in the hands of people who are a bit unsure of the answers. Even better is giving it to those who are *sure* they don't have the "final" answers, who know they are trying at best only to appoximate excellence, who know that the world is a lot bigger than their own current worldview. It is said that Teddy Roosevelt and a comrade who was a naturalist went outside on a clear night. After commenting on the size of the universe and the countless galaxies and stars, Roosevelt turned to his friend and said, "Okay, now we're small enough; we can go to bed."

Mix humility with a willingness to admit mistakes, and we have people who will use power to correct errors, improve operations, and develop a relentlessly improving function rather than to cover up their glitches. People expend vast quantities of power on hiding mistakes, especially when they themselves came up with, sold, or approved the idea. It's hard to admit the baby is ugly when it's your baby. Power given to those who will use it to protect their own hides is wasted.

We have to be careful not to be taken in by the illusion of humility. We want people who are genuinely aware of and accept their limitations no matter how talented they are. "[George] Washington had . . . proclaimed his own unworthiness since 1775, with such evident sincerity that his countrymen had showered powers on his head."[1]

One way to tell the difference between real and false humility is to watch how a person responds to defeat. The truly humble are those who have been defeated and quickly come back.

The falsely humble are those who have been defeated and never get over it.

"Humble" doesn't mean "not confident." Speaking at a writer's conference, I told those in attendance that the ideal attitude for writers is to have the confidence that they have something unique and worthwhile to say, and the humility to know that a lot of sweat and help from others can make it a whole lot better.

Honesty

For many of us, the longer we live, the more we appreciate the value of an honest comment and discount the value of flattery.

We should *never* give power to those who flatter us, butter us up, tell us how wonderful we are, say things to our faces that they would never say behind our backs. We want to put power into the hands of people who are honest, who don't just go along with something with which they disagree, who will challenge both old and new ideas, and who will call us on the carpet (*graciously* of course) if we're on the wrong track.

Who's the more valuable, the person who tells us that things are better than they really are, or the person who tells it like it is? Another question: Which one of these usually gets the better treatment in organizations (or in life, for that matter)? Your answer to the second question explains why there are so many rich liars. Wise leaders put the power where it will be used to advance truth rather than woo the organization to sleep.

Expansiveness

We should be very reluctant to give power to people who only talk about *their* area—their department, their operation, their function. These are the kind of people who mix power and politics, who see power primarily (or only) as a means of enhancing their own power base.

Much better are the people who have an expansive view, who are interested in and talk about other areas of the organization, other organizations, the industry or trade group, the economy and, at the high end, about things other than work and business. These people are much less likely to use any shared power in a limited manner. They might appear to be less focused (and we certainly don't want to give power to the unfocused), but we need to take the time to notice when the appearance is deceiving, when "unfocused" is really "focused on a bigger reality."

A potter in the Middle East had worked quietly but with intensity for many hours on one large water jar. He started, developed, stopped, started over, added to, and painstakingly honed his piece of work.

He began to attract an audience. First, children. Then a few women. Next, a town elder. Finally a crowd of people watched as the water jar took on a unique and majestic shape.

"Your work is very beautiful," said the elder. "But very inefficient. You have spent your whole day working on one jar. How can you justify that?"

The potter smiled but didn't look up. "It came into my heart to make a jar so special, so appealing, so refreshing in its appearance that if one of our generals a hundred years from now, parched and discouraged and on the verge of giving up, sees this jar, he will remember. That is why I am writing on the jar."

"What are you writing?" the elder asked, curious.

The potter looked up. He turned the jar slowly until the elder could read the word *remember.*

"Remember what?" the elder asked.

The potter resumed his work. "Remember that there is beauty. Remember that there is refreshment. Remember that a long time ago there was a potter who lived in a country where potters had the freedom to work inefficiently to make something worthy. And remember not to give up, and to fight hard for such a country."

The potter looked intently at the children, and then into the elder's eyes. "If it is good enough," he said, "this jar you see today in my hands might a hundred years

from now cause a discouraged man not yet born to stand
and fight again.

Now *that* is expansive.

A Relaxed Perspective

I would never give power to somebody who didn't have a sense
of humor. "Beware the man whose stomach moves not when he
laughs," warns an old Chinese proverb.

People who take themselves and the world too seriously are
among the most dangerous on the planet. People who don't
smile scare me. People whose definition of humor includes insults, sarcasm, and cynicism terrify me. Furrow-browed people
who think everything is broken and that they could fix it all if
only they had enough power—crusaders—make me want to go
into hiding.

We don't want to give power to the frivolous, but we do
want to give it to those who understand the time and place for
frivolity. People, the workplace, society at large, even the whole
world are often completely absurd. Power can't fix those things,
and using power to bring "order" (as imperialists, colonialists,
and empire builders have illustrated for centuries) often creates
even more absurdity, and usually a large amount of pain.

"Relaxed" does *not* mean "not intense." Intensity—doing
something with purpose, focus, and tenacity—is indispensable
for getting anything done. We want to give power to people who
can be intense. But we want these same people to know when
to let up, when to let go, when to stop. We want people who can
recognize when a great idea turns out to be a loser, and can
laugh their heads off rather than blow their heads off.

The world almost certainly needs prophets—serious people
who are willing to expend themselves in a worthy cause, who
are willing to sacrifice, who won't compromise no matter what.
We should honor these people. But if they don't know when to
laugh, we shouldn't give them any power.

And I'd *still* like it better if they could at least smile.

Savvy

Wielding power well will tax the abilities of anyone who tries it. To do it well requires savvy.

Savvy, or street smarts, is a hard-earned brew of mental intelligence, emotional intelligence, and common sense. It doesn't come automatically with age. "There's no fool like an old fool," we're told.

People with savvy know when to move and when to stop. When to talk and when to shut up. When to share an idea and when to protect it. When to fight and when to retreat. They won't waste power, but they won't miss an opportunity to use it, either. We pick them out by watching how they handle smaller situations and lower levels of power.

Savvy is different from *brilliance.* There are many brilliant people who don't know when to get out of the way of an oncoming train. Brilliant people can be disconnected, otherworldly, and pompous. Brilliant people are often granted power by virtue of their brilliance. They might make it work well.

But a brilliant person wielding destructive power? God help us.

A Concern for Justice

Fiorello LaGuardia, the mayor of New York from 1933 to 1945, once tried to convince the police to differentiate between criminal behavior and youthful pranks.

"When I was a boy," he told them seriously, "we would walk around until we found an unattended horse. We would ride him for a while and then bring him back to where he belonged."

"Are you telling us that the mayor of New York was once a horse thief?" one burly policeman asked incredulously.

"No," LaGuardia answered quietly. "I'm telling you that the mayor of New York was once a boy."[2]

We need to watch how people deal with others—with their colleagues, subordinates, suppliers, customers.

The free market is wonderful when it's bounded by some reasonable standards of social and economic justice and mercy. It's pretty terrifying when it's operating all alone under the law of *caveat emptor.* People operating in the same way are also pretty terrifying.

We need to give power to people who think win-win with other people and organizations—people who will use their power to help many over the long run rather than a few for the moment. Avoid giving power to the person who talks about "squeezing a little more" out of . . . whomever.

We need to powershare with people who think cooperation first and competition second, partnerships first and subordination second, turnaround first and termination second. Mostly, we need to powershare with people who think of justice first and of personal advantage as a result, not a goal.

Passion

If we're going to powershare with people, surely we hope that they'll *do* something with it.

Often, passionate people won't look like "safe" places to put power. Sometimes, they may seem to be a threat to our own position. But the reality is that in a dull, dusty-gray world, passionate people by their very nature already *possess* great power. And, as Thomas Moore writes, "it is foolish to deny signs of this power—individuality, eccentricity, self-expression, passion—because it cannot be truly repressed."[3]

When we're around these people, the sparks fly, the whole energy level goes up a notch. These people will speak and act with intensity, creativity, and a willingness to take things apart to make them better. They are already hard to lead; when we give them more power, they'll be even more difficult. This is so because life is always more challenging to direct than death.

If we won't honor these people of power with power, we can create a situation in which they will use whatever power they do have or can collect to do their own thing—or to do us in.

Granting Power Over People

When powersharing includes giving people authority over other people, the stakes go way up. Some of these stakes are:

- The development or destruction of people who may be linchpins of our future success

- The wise or foolish use of multiplied quantities of organizational resources
- Respect or disrespect for us and the organization, depending on how the power is used
- The clarification and achievement, or muddying and loss, of our organization's vision
- Enhanced individual performance if they powershare with others, lowered individual performance if they refuse to powershare

The key, again, is to start small. See how they do with one subordinate, particularly how they powershare with that subordinate. If they can't get it right with one, they'll be a disaster with ten or a hundred.

Then gradually increase their responsibility. For example, if the size of the organization warrants it, reward those who have been successful with one subordinate by giving them up to ten people to supervise. If they do well with these ten, let them lead five leaders who are each leading ten (total of fifty). Then let them lead ten who are each leading ten (total of a hundred). Finally, let them lead ten who are each leading a hundred (total of a thousand). Cracks can be seen before they become too large, and the person learns what works and doesn't work with a smaller pool of guinea pigs.

My ideal power candidates have at least a strong measure of all the characteristics discussed in this chapter.

Leave one out only at your peril.

Notes

1. Richard Brookhiser, *Founding Father: Rediscovering George Washington* (New York: Free Press, 1996), p. 102.
2. Clifton Fadiman, ed., *The Little, Brown Book of Anecdotes* (Boston: Little, Brown, 1985), pp. 339–340.
3. Thomas Moore, *Care of the Soul* (New York: HarperPerennial, 1994), p. 135.

14

The Other Side of the Balance: Keeping Power Out of the Wrong Hands

Power cannot be distributed equally. It may not be politically correct to say so, but some people don't deserve power. They're dangerous [and] they abuse it.

—Patricia Pitcher, *The Drama of Leadership,* p. 121

Power misused can produce horror unimaginable.

Hitler used power driven by racial hatred to kill six million Jews and to enslave most of Europe. Stalin used power driven by revenge and dictatorial impulses to kill countless Russians and to enslave the eastern half of Europe. Pol Pot used power driven by madly utopian ideas developed in Paris coffeehouses to exterminate 40 percent of the population of Cambodia.

As discussed in Chapter 12, power in organizations has been used inappropriately and unjustly to destroy other people's careers, other departments or divisions, competitors, suppliers, customers, and the organizations themselves. Unfettered by proper restraints and unleashed on an organization of any size, power has an immense capacity to visit disaster.

This disaster can take the form of:

- *Ignorance*—When power is used to keep people in the dark

- *Famine*—When power is used to keep needed truth, knowledge, or resources out of the minds that could feed on it
- *Drought*—When power is used to keep needed refreshment (rewards, recognition, comp time, sabbaticals) away from those who have spent themselves in the heat of the day.
- *Pestilence*—When power is used to spread uncontrollable viruses like slander, rumors, propaganda, and outright lies.
- *Civil War*—When power is used to create refugees (people who are forced to move).
- *Casualties*—When power is used to wound or terminate people because they're in the way.

The sad truth is that power is probably used more often— perhaps far more often—for these ends than for the ends of creativity, organizational development, meeting customers' needs, and justice. Our refusal to recognize this fact and to set boundaries around power provides its destructive form a ready-made playing field on which it can do its dirty work.

Power has to be attached to proper restraints. In saying this, I'm not talking about a detailed list of rules, or powersharing with the right "business units" (departments or divisions). Power is always in the hands of *individuals*—real, unique, living, breathing people—who can use it constructively or destructively. That's where the power will be, whether we design it that way and take pains to get it in the right hands, or let it "happen" and allow it to flow where it will—almost always into the wrong hands.

In preventing the abuse of power, the first and most important step is to keep it out of the wrong hands.

People Who Should Never Be Given Power

Aesop said, "Those who voluntarily put power into the hands of a tyrant or an enemy must not wonder if it be at last turned against themselves."

Making an accurate diagnosis of people as a means of properly powersharing with them is very difficult. People can be extremely creative in hiding who they are and what drives them. "This is why issues of power are so difficult to deal with: things are not as they appear to be. Weaklings puff themselves up and try to act strong; tough people hide their vulnerabilities; the rest of us fail to look past the surface. We assume that the fabrications of power all around us are genuine, and we fall victim to them."[1]

Despite the difficulty of recognizing power abusers, we must try. There are certain types of people who should never have power shared with them, and who may have to have what power they do have severely restricted or even withdrawn.

Before we discuss the different roles that destructive power can play, we need to clarify two points.

First, I am not saying that these kinds of people don't have power in organizations. On the contrary, they are often the norm. At times, the source of internal warfare may be several of these people "having it out" over the issue of their twisted power. Some small businesses are started by these types of people, people who want to use power in an abusive way and want to do it without interference; they may say they want to "be their own boss," but what they really mean is that they want to be *your* boss.

Second, this is not a chapter about "crazy bosses" (not because there aren't crazy bosses—there are many. I've worked for a few). But some of these bosses grew crazy in part as a result of their continual, perverted use of power; they "practiced up" in their earlier, smaller roles. Others just did a good job of hiding their craziness until they had a power base.

The point here is that anyone can abuse power because everyone has power, at the very least the power to destroy. You don't have to be in formal authority or very high up the organization chart to exercise it. From production line workers who contaminate product to mail room clerks who deliberately lose mail, from purchasing assistants who don't report overbillings to customer service contacts who pass their bad day along to their customers, destructive power can show up anywhere.

Let's get a feel for the worst.

Dictators

Some people are dictating machines. They simply like the "buzz" they get from being in total control.

The problem is this: If the main reason they want power is to be exhilarated by it, the only way for them to get excited is by aquiring more power. They become power absorbers, self-aggrandizers who seek out and possess every speck of power that enters their field of vision. Power can become a drug, and the lust for it insatiable.

The clue is to look at what people do with their power. If they use it to become dictators—people who use power to dictate what they desire regardless of the negative impact on people or goals, or regardless of its validity—we need to keep power far away from them. Using power to get power and then get more power, and considering power as a base of operations rather than as a tool to be used, are clear signals that an abuse of power is in motion.

"The . . . overly ambitious type [is] the absolute worst choice in the company," warns leadership author Robert Townsend. "This type of person wants power, needs power, and can't live without power. He is authoritarian, insensitive, and careless of others."[2] There is a great divide between those who are selfishly ambitious and those who ambitiously seek the betterment of the organization, its stakeholders, and—as a by-product—themselves.

One of the classic tools of dictators is unpredictability. Sometimes they're in a bad mood, sometimes a good (or at least better) mood. Which mood exists at the moment is not foreseeable or explainable by reason or logic. They like to keep other people off balance. They want others to have to come back to them repeatedly for information and decisions. There can be no interdependence with a dictator or in a dictatorial environment. Only dependence on them.

"Don't give power to people who can't live without it," said U.S. Secretary of State George Schultz.[3]

Controllers

Where dictators are perverse leaders, controllers are perverse managers.

Where dictators have visions (read: nightmares) and want you to do whatever they want and can think up next, controllers have an old blueprint and want you to follow it—period. Both want power to manipulate others, and both can want the same quantity of power. They just apply it in different ways. Dictators are more creative, keep people off balance, and rely on fear to make people feel tiny. Controllers are more comprehensive, keep people in line, and rely on fear to make people feel stupid.

Controllers use any available power to chain people. They often really believe that success will come only if their perfect rules and procedures are perfectly followed. The first problem, of course, is that there are no perfect rules and procedures. The second problem is that there are no people who can—or will—perfectly follow them. And the third problem is that the procedures may not be worth following in the first place. They add no value.

Controllers are micromanagers who, for reasons of their own personal development, have a need to exercise tight-fisted control of their environment. Often, it's to make up for an inner life that's out of control ("I can't control me, so I'll control you instead"). Power granted to them will be used only to fuel their insatiable drive to bring everything around them "under control." The power will usually be wasted, even in *that* unexemplary endeavor.

And God help us if it isn't wasted, and they succeed.

Technocrats

"That won't work," Sean said sternly. "Our customers will never buy it."

"How do you know that?" Joe asked, struggling to keep the resentment out of his voice.

"I've read the research. And the major industry trendspotters point in the same direction."

Joe, a twenty-year marketing manager with in-depth experience with these very customers, could no longer restrain himself. "Have you ever," he asked angrily, "even talked with one of our customers about this idea?"

"Don't need to," Sean answered, unperturbed. "I've got the data."

Technocrats are experts at dissecting other people's dreams, visions, goals, and plans. They don't use their power to create and build, only to analyze and critique. They can sound positively brilliant in their comments and insights, but we can't afford to be seduced by their reasoning capacity, no matter how gigantic it is.

We have to listen carefully to discern whether this person ever uses power constructively and positively. Critical analysis is an excellent skill, but it is a deadly extreme when it is the *only* skill. Then, all of its power is used to dissect and disagree and oppose.

And I'm not just talking about listening to the words they speak. It's what they do with them. In Patricia Pitcher's words, "[They] have all the vocabulary of imagination and listening, but . . . they're rigid and dogmatic and cold and calculating, and they don't listen to anybody. *Leading* is about putting them in their place."[4] In short, *we* have to listen to hear how well *they* listen.

And if they don't listen, we must not give them any power.

Unforgivers

Unforgivers believe that forgiveness is a "church" thing, something that is soft, silly, and inappropriate in an organizational setting. This view is horrifyingly cold and harsh.

There are those who will use power to abuse others who make mistakes. They can criticize and limit and, especially if they perceive the mistake as an offense against them personally, cut the mistaken person right out of organizational existence.

Power should never be used this way, and those who do aren't fit candidates for power. If the mistakes are deliberate or repetitively stupid, the offender should be disciplined or terminated; no abuse is necessary. If the mistakes are derived from the more usual sources—because the offenders didn't know what to do, because they had insufficient training, because they tried something new and it didn't work, because they are fragile and fallible—then abuse is not only the wrong answer, it's unjust and a disciplinable error in its own right.

This abuse carried out by unforgivers can be overt, coming in the form of harsh reviews, verbal floggings, humiliation in front of peers, demotions, or pay cuts. But it can also be quite subtle. One of the most common subtle forms is the creation of rigid rules in an attempt to ensure that the mistake isn't repeated. The problem is that creativity and risk also won't be repeated.

It's a good idea to review the past and learn from it—as long as we learn the right things. But when the "learning" takes the form of elongating the procedure manual, we're almost certainly heading in the wrong direction. Governments and large bureaucracies tend to do this almost reflexively. Some people thrive on "plugging up" the messy little holes that people, being people, seem constantly to find or make. Mistakes can too easily be used as an excuse to disempower people.

Everyone makes mistakes. Beware of the people who are willing to throw stones at others but are unwilling to admit their own frail humanity.

Keeping a list of errors made by others isn't generally a healthy thing to do. But it might be appropriate to keep track of the errors made by unforgivers.

They need help remembering they came off the same production line as everyone else.

Vetoers

All too often, opposition political parties fail when they finally get into power. They've spent so long developing and honing their negative program that they've forgotten (or never realized) that we can't run anything of value for very long on negative energy. "You can't beat something with nothing," advises the old political adage.

There are many who will use power to slow down progress and maintain the status quo. "We've always done it this way" is their battle cry.

But maintaining the status quo is not a positive endeavor, because everything in life can be improved. Rigidity requires using power to kill new ideas in their infancy, to overhighlight the flaws in suggestions, to build alliances to hurt or damage others' plans, and to overemphasize the importance of one's own convenience and stability. The power to veto can at times be useful and constructive, but more often it is used to stop progress in its tracks.

Vetoers will use power to build elaborate walls of defense against truth and reality. Erecting multiple levels of approval is one of their favorite techniques. "Ways to say no proliferate. The kind of changes that survive an approval chain of fourteen signatures will not be the bold experiments or quick responses needed."[5] We need to pay attention to those who make others jump through hoops to get the required blessing.

The easiest thing in the world is to boo (it may be one of the prime reasons for the existence of sports). But using organizational power to boo is a waste or worse. We may want someone who boos as a staff adviser to keep us honest, but we have to be very careful not to powershare with them beyond their advisory role.

Hearing the word *no* starts early. Researchers have estimated that children may hear from eight to twelve noes for every yes. People are used to being stopped. "I think the one lesson probably all CEOs need to learn," concludes Ken Lay, "is, you have to be very reluctant to tell somebody they shouldn't do something."[6]

Vetoers, on the contrary, are eager to say no.

Suppressors

There are some who will use their power to suppress the truth.

This suppression can take several forms. It can be used to hide information that could hurt the suppressor or one of her projects if it became known. All of us can succumb to this temptation, especially if the news is particularly obnoxious, but some do it as a way of life. This is the "CYA" syndrome, and it can too easily become a person's top priority.

This tool can also be used to suppress favorable truth about others who are viewed as competitors. In this case, suppressors aren't really out to make others look bad so much as they are out to keep others from looking good. Beware the leaders who are sparing in their praise of others.

"No system should give those with more authority the power to silence the people below them."[7] Power can be used to open channels of communication or to close them. Suppressors are abusers who deposit plaque in the organization's arteries.

We have to scrape them out before the body dies.

Deceivers

Some people will use power to weave illusions about themselves, their areas of responsibility, their successes, and their failures.

They use power to create lies on the one hand and to obliterate truth on the other. They believe that if they are just clever enough, strategic enough, and forceful enough, their deficiencies can be hidden or, at the highest level of deceit, be made to look like successes. They masquerade as the good and true to cover up a reality of problems and lies. They put on a good front of honesty and perhaps even humility, but by their actions deny the power of real truth.

Some examples:

- A production supervisor who reported some types of scrap as inventory, in the process reducing his scrap rates while inflating his inventory levels
- An accounting department manager at a remote location who relabeled obsolete, useless inventory to exaggerate the asset list
- A senior purchasing executive who selectively got key suppliers to accept lower unit prices (on which he was measured) and to transfer the costs to other areas like handling, restocking, and technical support (which he was not measured on)
- A CEO who "cooked the books" when presenting them to his people "open-book management" style, giving them a performance picture worse than it was in reality in an attempt to scare and push them

Deceivers are excellent at making one thing look like another. They can, for example, make the disagreement of others look like disloyalty, and their own quiet acquiescence to long-term (but hard-to-see) harmful decisions look like loyalty. They are masters at creating false impressions. At their best, deceivers can transform something before our eyes into its very opposite.

We have to realize that a deception carried on with vigor for a long enough period becomes believable to the deceiver. One of the horrible circumstances of using power to deceive is that such people end up deceiving themselves.

Our solution is not to try to "crack" the lie, to continue trying to get the person to see the truth long after it's become apparent that it's not an information or education problem. Deceivers need to be stripped of power, and probably of their positions as well.

Scapegoaters

"When a man blames others for his failures, it's a good idea to credit others with his successes," said Howard W. Newton.

Scapegoaters are pretenders.

They pretend, first, that they have no responsibility. "It's not my job," "That's not my area," "I didn't know," "I didn't mean that." It's easier to pin a tail on a donkey than to pin responsibility on a jackass.

They pretend, second, that they have no power. They are "victims" who couldn't have done anything to prevent the problem. "I don't see what I should have done differently." "What could I do?" "I didn't feel that I was in a position to jump in there." "Surely nobody thinks its *my* fault, do they?" It's a front of helplessness. Don't believe it.

What they *do* do is use their power to delegate blame. They can use massive amounts of time and energy—critical components of power—to shift the blame onto others. They claim to be victims, which they are not, but they end up creating true victims, people who really didn't do what they're being blamed for. At its worst, whole groups of people have been scapegoated and eliminated.

Examples:

• An advertising department in a large organization was blamed by marketing for a failed campaign. The truth? The marketing people had withheld crucial information from the advertising department and had insisted on the inclusion of several failed portions of the campaign.

• A vice president of finance was fired for securing loans that nearly bankrupted the company. Why had he done so? Because he was directed to by the CEO.

• A project manager was fired after a failed proposal on a major new project, and the vice president of business development, after criticizing the project manager, was given more control of the proposal process. The reality? The elements of the proposal that lost the project were the brainchild of the vice president.

• Countless team leaders have blamed their teams' failures on members whom they know will never get a hearing. Why? They want to hide the fact that the problems were actually failures of leadership.

Scapegoaters are miserable repositories of power. Listen carefully for the sounds of the ugly words "It's their fault." If you hear them, disempower.

Subversives

A subversive is a rebel without a cause.

Rebels can be good for an organization when they rebel against mindless goals, outmoded processes, restrictive procedures, and useless work. Rebelling against the ineffective to pave the way for the effective deserves a medal rather than a firing squad (although it usually seems to get the latter).

Subversives are rebels without a good organizational cause. Where honest rebels disobey for the good of the organization, subversives disobey for the good of themselves. They aren't trying to upset a bogus "authority" (such as a rule); rather, they're trying to establish a new authority (that is, themselves). "The worst disorder in an army occurs, not when the privates mutiny, but when the officers do. Officers . . . are used to wielding power. If they disobey, it is not to overturn authority, but to assume it."[8]

We have to look closely at those who seem to chafe under authority, especially when it is a repetitive pattern. The honest rebels at times need to be treated with benign neglect and at other times with respect and more power. The subversives at all times must be restrained, limited, and disempowered.

Both rebels and subversives talk about making things better. The question we have to ask is, "For whom?"

Killers

Much of literature addresses the theme of the person who uses his power to shed the blood of others. While this still literally happens today, the far more common occurrence is the shedding of blood in a figurative way (including damaging another's reputation, withholding crucial information that allows a project to sink, or not giving credit where credit is due).

There are two main driving forces behind this use of power. One is "blind ambition," a drive for personal recognition and rewards to the exclusion of every other observable goal. Life is viewed as a zero-sum game: "If you have it, then I can't, so I'll have to take it if I want it." Watch out for the person who can't tell the difference between healthy competition and diseased warfare.

The second driving force is revenge, the planning and plotting of the demise of another person or group because of damage done in the past, whether the damage is real or only perceived or imagined. Even though many of its applications are incredibly petty, we shouldn't underestimate the destructive power of revenge. We have to beware of people who put others on the spot, who try to look good at the expense of others, who talk about others in the organization in "enemy" terms. We don't have to guess how they'll use any power we give them.

Or how they'll treat us someday.

A Final Caution

Good intentions about powersharing with our people are worth a lot, but they're not sufficient to ensure success.

Even when our purposes are good, power can cause unintended negative consequences. "Power, no matter how well-intentioned, tends to cause suffering," writes ethicist Philip Yancey.[9] Power always changes things, and it can be very hard to predict all of the changes—and impossible to control all of their effects. What this means to us is that even getting power into the best of hands won't necessarily eliminate major problems.

But we can take appropriate steps to control our distribution of power and to prevent its abuse, which can at least minimize its negative effects. We can powershare with great discrimination and disempower when the evidence demands it. Anything less puts our organizations at great risk of failure.

We have to remember that these people can keep coming back like Dracula to harm us or others in our organizations. These power abusers seldom change, except to become more subtle in their methods. "For us, [getting rid of abusive managers] meant ushering out several dozen leaders," says Mort Meyerson, chairman and CEO of Perot Systems. "Though they had met or exceeded their financial goals, they mistreated the people under them. . . . That very difficult step made us a better company immediately."[10]

May we be able to say about power abusers, as the ancient Hebrew King Solomon did long ago, "All they expected from their power came to nothing."

We'll have to pay attention and take strong action to make it so.

Notes

1. Thomas Moore, *Care of the Soul* (New York: HarperPerennial, 1994), p. 130.
2. Warren Bennis and Robert Townsend, *Reinventing Leadership* (New York: William Morrow, 1995), p. 154.

3. As quoted by Warren Bennis in *Reinventing Leadership,* p. 14.
4. Patricia Pitcher, *The Drama of Leadership* (New York: Wiley, 1997), p. 6.
5. Gifford and Elizabeth Pinchot, *The Intelligent Organization* (San Francisco: Berrett-Koehler Publishers, 1994, 1996), p. 18.
6. Ken Lay, as quoted in Gary Hamel, "Turning Your Business Upside Down," *Fortune,* 23 June 1997, p. 88.
7. Pinchot, *The Intelligent Organization,* p. 91.
8. Richard Brookhiser, *Founding Father: Rediscovering George Washington* (New York: Free Press, 1996), p. 39.
9. Philip Yancey, *The Jesus I Never Knew* (Grand Rapids, Mich.: Zondervan Publishing House, 1995), p. 205.
10. "Lessons in Leadership: Perot Systems's Mort Meyerson Speaks Out," *Bottom Line Personal,* 1 October, 1997, p. 13.

15

Finding the Quality Balance Through Power Allocation

Real liberty is neither found in despotism or the extremes of democracy, but in moderate governments.

—Alexander Hamilton

Few tasks are as daunting for a leader as the attempt to maximize constructive power and minimize destructive power (we can't eliminate it).

Because it's so difficult to do well, and possibly because it's such a messy, unquantifiable activity, many leaders simply avoid thinking about it deeply. Instead, they make the "obvious" decisions:

- "Give that to Donna. She's got more experience than anyone on that topic."
- "That is definitely a marketing issue. Let's kick that decision to them."
- "I know Marc hasn't done very well in getting his people on board, but he's got the credentials to get that project done. Just tell him he needs to delegate more."
- "I'd love to get around those empire builders in purchasing and let you buy this directly. I know you could save us some real money and maybe even more headaches. But they'd have my head."

Wrestling With the Balance

Most of us must wrestle constantly with how to get things done. But in a world of interconnected (and often disconnected) human beings, the wrestling is escalated as we search for a reasonable and workable balance of power.

Interdependent leaders have to struggle to find a balance between using their power and sharing their power if they want to achieve maximum overall effectiveness. And then they have to grapple with the question of who is worthy of powersharing with them.

But it's the wrestling, the struggling, and doubting that lead our organizations to true interdependence and redeem the value and use of power. Power itself doesn't corrupt, but power in the wrong hands always does, whether it's in the hands of a power abuser or is simply misplaced in impotent or unqualified hands.

The margins of success today are very narrow. We can't powershare with people who won't use it interdependently. We need to keep it away from those who use it for their own ends, hoard it, or use it to build little fiefdoms. We need to get it into the hands of those who use it for *building*—building others up, building teams, building the future of the organization.

Steps to Finding the Quality Balance

The result we're looking for is a powerful organization. Intelligent powersharing that recognizes both the need for interdependence and the need for quality power allocation is the means.

Finding this quality balance requires us to take the time to go through an eight-step process.

Step 1: Ask the Right Questions

The key to enhancing constructive power in organizations while driving out destructive power is to powershare with the right people and disempower the wrong people. The first step in doing so is to ask ourselves some important questions:

- Why does this person want more power? What are her real motives?
- Where can this power do the most good? How do I get it there?
- Where would it do the most harm? How do I keep it out of there?
- How has he used power in the past? Has he used it for building? Does his usage reflect any history of abuse?
- What do those who have worked around this person say about her use of power?
- What is the atmosphere around this person? Is there positive energy? Is there fear? Are other people fresh and open or downcast and closed?
- Is this person primarily positive or negative? Does he frame discussions and presentations in upbeat or cynical terms?
- Does this person have a positive agenda? Or does she govern more by criticism and veto?
- Is this person concerned enough about people? Is he more interested in people or things?
- Is this person using power to set expectations, stir great effort, or stand against bad ideas?
- Is this person using power to convey a vision or values, to give them form through the use of organizational stories, and to persuade others to sign up with their hearts and minds?
- Is this person using power to define the organization's function and form, understand people's aspirations and tie them to organizational goals, and paradoxically expand the possibilities while narrowing the focus?
- What do this person's words and metaphors say about her? Does she talk abut cooperation and mutually beneficial effort? Or does she talk about "us versus them" and winning? Does she quote Confucius or Genghis Khan?

My own experience tells me that we have to force ourselves to ask these questions and have them answered as clearly as possible before we allocate power. Cutting short this interrogatory phase is a formula for wasted and probably abusive power.

Step 2: Face Our Fears and Concerns About People

People are never going to be "ready" for powersharing.

They'll never be smart enough, good enough, experienced enough, trustworthy enough. They'll do the wrong thing a lot. Sometimes, they won't even be sorry about it. They'll take up our time and attention and training and then give us two weeks' notice. Some might even try to stab us in the back.

People can be a miserable lot.

But we can look at all the flaws and reach the erroneous conclusion that people are no good. "No good deed goes un-punished." "Give them an inch and they'll take a mile." "Those people are dead from the neck up." We'll design a structure that includes jail cells and straightjackets. We'll be tempted to maim and kill.

A constructively powerful leader builds an organization on personal trustworthiness (that's our side, and that's the charac-ter part) and on trusting others to do the right thing (that's their side, and that's the crazy part). Actual trust is earned by being trustworthy, but we'll have to trust people at some level even before they've earned it—even though it is, in a sense, ridiculous to trust.

It's a big risk. We have to design a structure that will mini-mize that risk.

And then we have to take it.

Step 3: Match Carefully

We have to be very careful when matching people to assign-ments. This is particularly important in two cases, promotions and assigning people to teams.

When we promote someone to a position of formal author-ity, we are making an embodied statement about our views on powersharing. Promote a controller, and people will read into it that we and our organization value control. With promotions, we are also making a long-term commitment to a specific and substantial form of powersharing with a specific individual, who can use or abuse that commitment and can be very hard to dislodge if abusive. A lot of decisions must be made quickly. Promotions should never be among them.

Probably nothing is more important or has less time spent on it than the decision of who the members of a team should be. "The uniqueness of each team member," asserts Ray Palmer, "is both a strength and a deterrent to success."[1]

And that's only part of the problem. Put any of the abusers discussed in Chapter 14 on a team and watch the team atrophy or explode. Dictators will dominate, destroying creativity and openness. Vetoers will boo, derailing progress and replacing it with frustration. Deceivers will hide their real agendas, making team conversations awkward and team decisions strained. Make no mistake—a team *cannot* achieve great things with an abuser aboard. The wrong mix of people makes destructive power—and the resultant dependence or independence—close to inevitable.

Step 4: Consider Character, Not Credentials

We have to decide to grant power on the basis of goals and motivations rather than position or credentials. We can't allow ourselves to assume that people will just do the "right thing" with an allocation of power. We have to *know* what they're going to do with it, at least in general terms, and then monitor them closely enough to detect if they are among the power abusers.

It was the curse of many earlier ages to substitute position for character, as in arguments based on the "divine right of kings" or "because I'm the boss, that's why." It is the curse of our own age to substitute credentials for character, as in "They've got the final say because they've got the _____ [*degree, license, certification, past experience, financial clout*]." People should have the *final* say—the power to make decisions—only when they've got something *constructive* to say.

We have to pay special attention to their commitment to truth by evaluating what they think, say, and do. People who play fast and loose with the truth, and people who are self-deceived, are disastrous repositories of power. Along with this, we should try to discern their ability to transform truth into wisdom so that the constructive effects of their use of power will be magnified.

Step 5: Encourage and Train

Some will fear the power we give them and will be reluctant to use it, especially if they've never had power before, have been wounded by other people using it against them, or were burned when they tried to use it themselves. These people, who aren't seeking power on the one hand, and understand both its and their own limitations on the other, may be the safest people with whom to powershare. But as we acknowledge and welcome their weaknesses, we need to show them the way to negate those weaknesses through interdependence.

If people don't want to powershare—to use their skills, take responsibility, be accountable, own problems, add value— regardless of our best efforts to involve them, we have to let them go. Every person today has to fully count.

Step 6: Share Power Unevenly

We've got to give it soonest and in the largest quantities to those who have the character to use it wisely. Powersharing isn't a program or initiative or event. It's a painstaking process.

And we've got to allow for individuality. "The lesson is to let individuals be themselves—no matter what their identity," said Phil Jackson, coach of the frequent world-champion Chicago Bulls. "The bottom line is whether they work hard and produce for the team."[2]

Step 7: Evaluate Regularly

Watch what people do with the power they already have. There's no better clue as to what they will do with more. If they abuse it, we need to take it away, push them to the side, box them in, limit their impact, and move them out of the organization if necessary. Listen especially to the people who work below them and around them. Some of the worst abusers of power smile and shine when working with their superiors, and direct all their abuse at their followers and peers.

If they handle power well, constructively and interdepen-

Exhibit 15-1. Questions relevant to allocating power.

Question	Yes	No	Unsure
1. Does this person readily acknowledge his need of help?			
2. Is this person able to work effectively even when not in a position of power?			
3. Does this person seek out and listen to diverse sources of information and knowledge?			
4. Would this person ever voluntarily lay down power?			
5. Does this person have a flexible view of power, and know that there will be an ebb and flow to leading and following?			
6. Does this person automatically begin powersharing in any new assignment or position?			
7. Can this person deal comfortably and patiently with ambiguous situations?			
8. Does this person use power to protect, forgive, and heal rather than to dissect, accuse, and wound others?			
9. Is this person aware of her fallibility, always improving her answers, and willing to admit her mistakes?			
10. Does this person quickly rally after a failure or defeat?			
11. Will this person tell me the truth, even if it hurts—me *or* them?			
12. Is this person interested in things other than his position or specific work area, especially things outside of work?			

Question	Yes	No	Unsure
13. Does this person have a sense of humor and know when and how to use it to diffuse difficult or tense situations?			
14. Does this person have the savvy to know when to use and when to lose power?			
15. Is this person just and fair in her dealings with colleagues and stakeholders?			
16. Does this person think in terms of win-win rather than win-lose?			
17. Is this person excited and passionate about what he is doing?			

dently, we need to give them more freedom and let them exercise more of their power.

Step 8: Seek Advice

It would be very useful to have advisers to assist us in powersharing judiciously. This could be a "no baloney" person who works for us or alongside us. Or it could be someone we trust outside the organization who has both access to enough information to give us accurate advice and enough real-world experience to give us workable advice.

Distributing power is so important and so hard to do well over time that we need all the good advice we can get.

Some important questions to ask yourself when allocating power to anyone are given in Exhibit 15-1.

Any noes to these questions should make us hesitate in allocating power. Three or more? Not on your life.

Or in this life.

Notes

1. Ray Palmer, "Assessing Virtual Teams," paper presented at the Greater Kansas City ASTD conference, 29 March, 1996, p. 2.
2. As quoted in *Bottom Line Personal,* 15 January, 1997, p. 14.

16

Conquering the Factors That Inhibit Constructive Power

Isn't it curious that most managers think empowerment can be done effortlessly, with little information and training and no clear relationship to business goals? Wishing doesn't make it so.

—Barbara Ettorre, "The Empowerment Gap: Hype vs. Reality," *Management Review,* July/August 1997, p. 11

There are a number of factors that can work against our constructive use of power. They can reduce our voice to a raspy whisper.

In this chapter, we'll look first at the factors that are internal to our organization, and then move on to those that are external. We'll suggest some solutions along the way.

Internal Factors

What are some of the key internal inhibiting factors? Seven stand out.

Unidimensional Communication

Many organizations are characterized by one-way forms of communication. Reports go up. Directives come down. The people on top don't really know what's going on in the organization, and the people down the line don't know where the organization is going. A lot of apparent communication is happening, but no *real* communication is taking place. The word *communication* itself means "a sending, giving, or exchanging of information, ideas, etc." This includes both the transmission of the idea and its two-way exchange. Perhaps a better word would be *conversation,* which means "talk, especially informal and friendly; good talk practiced as an art; exploratory discussion of an issue."

It is much easier to use power destructively than constructively. Only through frequent, voluminous, multidimensional conversation can we together find the way to constructive power.

Suggested Solution: We need to say yes immediately to proposed or ongoing conversations, and to take a long time before we say no. This includes conversation between different levels of authority, different departments or divisions, and people inside every part of our organization with people inside every part of our customers' and suppliers' organizations. We need some guidelines to prevent duplicate or contradictory efforts. Our attitude, though, should be that we'd rather have unchartable, untrackable conversations and deal with the problems stemming from them than have no conversation and no untidy problems—or creativity, or solutions—at all.

Either/Or Boundaries

People do need to have some boundaries in order to manage themselves and function effectively. Everybody can't do everything, and everyone can't be available to everyone else at all times. There can be some similarities between an open-door system and an open-sewer system. But unidimensional, either/or boundaries (for example, "either purchasing will perform this task or production will"; "either this group will work on this product line or that one will") rigidly established and enforced reduce the constructive power available to capitalize on an opportunity or to resolve a problem.

Suggested Solution: Blur the dividing *walls* on the way to turning them into *hedges.* Use cross-functional (that is, barrier-smashing) teams whenever possible. Move people for extended periods into departments or functions that match their personality/interests/values chart to give them a multidimensional perspective. Use brief "student exchange" programs to give people a firsthand understanding of the glory and the shame of other areas. Insist that any innovations be shared quickly and widely so that no one gets an "edge" on anyone else. Assign pieces of a project to different groups and let them sort out the plan of cooperation—or go down together.

Halfway Downsizing

In many reductions in force, people are eliminated, but the work just goes on and on. Often, the work load actually increases. The people left behind can become overloaded, burned out, and virtually incapable of responding to, much less using, constructive power.

Suggested Solution: When faced with a necessary reduction of staff, we need to use our power not just to eliminate positions but to eliminate *activity.* It's not realistic or reasonable to say, "We still need all the work, we just don't need the people who are doing it." The best efforts here will actually reduce work load by *more* than the staff is reduced so that the remaining people will have the time and freedom from stress to find new ways to meet customer needs and add value.

Staff Dominance

People in staff positions (such as advisory, counseling, or forecasting positions) can be stunning inhibitors of constructive power. When we let them work on many projects at a time without ever finishing any, when we don't measure the value (if any) of their activity, and allow them to overrule and even rule line people (that is, decision-making, operating people), they can be-

come the organizational equivalent of road construction during
rush hour.

Suggested Solution: Track staff productivity over time and
insist that it go up *faster* than operating productivity. Do this by
insisting that at any one period of time they work on only a small
number of value-adding projects that have specific, measurable
results. Require them to support rather than to dominate or interfere with line people (we'll have to verify this in detail with
the line people). Never let people work in a staff position who
haven't had to get their hands dirty and prove that they can do a
good job of it. And never hire or develop "professional" staff,
people who make a career out of staff work. If you have any staff
empires, lay siege to them quickly and starve them out.

Absence of Veto

Although we classified the "vetoer" as a power abuser in Chapter
14, that doesn't void the fact that an absence of a clear and willingly used veto will limit constructive power. "That the veto is
built into systems of government at the highest level—United
Nations Security Council, the American presidency—shows a
profound recognition of the importance of negativity and suggests that negation is fundamental to the power of power."[1]
Without a veto, wild and wasteful ideas can run amok, absorbing
the constructive power of the organization.

Suggested Solution: Build a limited veto (one that affects
certain kinds or levels of decision) into the operating policy and
culture. Take pains to make sure that everyone understands that
it's a positive tool that will be used to keep the organization focused. And make sure it's a true veto; allow it to be overridden if
there is a preset level of sentiment in that direction. There will
still be some major decisions outside the veto system, but all
those within it should be subject to the give-and-take of decision-
veto override.

Orphan Problems

Constructive power can be left unapplied in important situations
because no one "owns" the problem at hand. We can't just ex-

pect that whenever a problem appears, "somebody" will take the responsibility for attacking it. The old maxim holds: When everybody is responsible for everything, then nobody is responsible for anything.

Suggested Solution: Take steps to ensure that there are no orphan problems. Note the problems that are festering in the cracks between people, teams, or departments. Although many people may be needed to effect the solution, make sure the leadership of the problem-solving effort is clear and unequivocal. Allow volunteer leadership whenever possible—because the people who volunteer are the most likely to stay with it until it is conquered. Reward and recognize people for taking problem ownership, and penalize those who dodge it, either by reducing their opportunities or by allocating unpleasant but clear-cut problems to them.

Exclusiveness

Exclusiveness can take many forms. We're overly protective of our discoveries, knowledge, or information. We make it hard to break into the "inner circle." We believe that our way is the best way. Whatever the form, exclusiveness prevents power from being constructively used by the group with others, or by others with the group.

Suggested Solution: Build into the culture the reality that there is no "one way" or "best way." Whatever we know is built on the work of others, and at best will be a building block into the future. We need to really absorb the principle of diversity, not just because it's right (which it is) but because it's the way to a bigger future rather than a smug present.

External Factors

There are also some external factors that can work against our application of constructive power.

Consuming Customers

The customer isn't always right. Sometimes they're wrong. Sometimes they're just plain horrible. Nothing can soak up an organization's power faster or more completely than a demanding, persistent, obnoxious customer. Customers are hard to come by, but some of them should be easy to let go. We have to remember the truth that whatever a nasty customer is complaining about when they come to us, they'll be saying about us when they leave.

Suggested Solution: Develop the organizational mind-set that the customer is important but not supreme. Measure customers' actual contribution to profitability and future growth and make sure you look at all the costs attached to that customer, including the extra time spent by marketing, sales, customer service, technical support, inventory operations, and so on. Finally, perform an annual anonymous survey of your employees to determine who the stinkers are and to discern whether any of the customers are so bad that they should be fired. Make sure you include the question: "If this was your business, which customer, if any, would you fire?"

Ineffective Suppliers

Suppliers should be a powerful extension of the organization, not a crippling appendage. The amount of time and effort spent on dealing with, correcting, fighting with, and making allowances for poor and mediocre suppliers can be astonishing.

Suggested Solution: Evaluate suppliers annually. Eliminate the poor suppliers immediately and give the mediocre suppliers a limited-time performance improvement plan. Insist that suppliers upgrade their capability continuously and supply technical expertise as well as product. Include suppliers on cross-functional teams and flunk the ones who contribute nothing. Finally, use the annual anonymous survey of your own people to weed out any suppliers that your "experts" miss.

Absorbing Alliances

This really is a time for strategic alliances—joining forces with other organizations to gain marketplace advantage and innovative synergy. But it absorbs a lot of power. In some cases, it's like managing a whole new department or division; in others, it's like managing a whole new business. "A trusting relationship, complementary products or services, and similar corporate cultures are important—but they aren't enough to make an alliance succeed. You have to manage the details, too."[2] Managing the details can use up a lot of power; *not* managing the details can consume even more.

Suggested Solution: Go beyond the potential gains and synergies to look at the probable costs and limitations that an alliance will bring. Ask yourself: What will it *really* cost us to make this alliance productive? Will it slow down our product development? Will it limit our channels of distribution? How likely are we to have to spend our power on damage control and the salvaging of a formerly good customer or supplier? Evaluate alliances annually, and clear out, in a face-saving way, the ones that are consuming your energies.

Absence of Focus

In a world of mergers, acquisitions, creativity, and new-product and new-service initiatives, we can easily find our constructive power thinned out as we aim our efforts at a hundred targets. The same level of power that might achieve fabulous results in a few major arenas can evaporate without impact if the field is too large.

Suggested Solution: Some have suggested that we "stick to our knitting." But that moves us too far back in the other direction. We have to branch out, to find new ideas related to the knitting, to expand the impact of our power by channeling it along parallel rivulets. We have to have alternative ideas ready in case knitting becomes unprofitable or obsolete. We have to recognize that we might not want to do some forms of knitting, and that we can't knit everything that needs to be knitted. And we need to stick with something long enough to verify that it really is, or isn't, a reasonable offshoot of our knitting.

Just as we need to work individually without distraction for thirty to sixty minutes to get into "flow" (where we're thinking clearly and deeply about the issue at hand), so we need to work for some focused, uninterrupted period of time on an idea to see if it is a valid user of our constructive power.

Image

We can spend a vast amount of constructive power trying to build a positive image or shake a negative one. In all this, we can forget that the best use of constructive power is to do something of value for multiple stakeholders. Often, the more we press to be thought of highly, the bigger becomes the gap with our performance reality; the more we press to lose a negative image, the more our stakeholders think we "protest too much."

Suggested Solution: Do the right thing, do the best thing, and let the image take care of itself over the long haul. "As hard as it is to believe now, there was a time when [Michael] Jordan was thought to be all style and no substance, that he would win scoring titles (he now has nine) but not NBA titles because he could not elevate the play of his teammates."[3] Jordan didn't spend his power on efforts to improve his image. He spent it on toughening himself and his teammates and focusing on winning. The image took care of itself.

●

One additional factor brings us back to the second section of this book: a shortage of power. Too little power—power less than what is needed to accomplish a goal or less than a person is equipped to handle—causes a severe limitation of constructive power. It's akin to the failure of an undercapitalized business. When power drops to a level where people feel helpless, discouragement can take over, blinding the powerless to their own possibilities and limiting the future viability of the organization.

Constructive power can certainly be canceled out by destructive power. But we have also seen that it can be drained away by other factors that are within our control. If we limit the factors, we'll magnify our constructive power.

And our results.

Notes

1. James Hillman, *Kinds of Power: A Guide to Its Intelligent Use* (New York: Currency Doubleday, 1995), p. 196.
2. Donna Fenn, "Details, Details, Detail," *Inc.,* July 1997, p. 107.
3. Phil Taylor, "To the Top," *Sports Illustrated,* 23 June, 1997, p. 32.

17

Conquering the Factors That Breed Destructive Power

Power invariably means both responsibility and danger.
—Theodore Roosevelt

There are factors both internal and external to the organization that can work to breed and grow destructive power. It's very important that we be aware of these incubators of horror.

As we look at these, we'll also offer some possible cures.

Internal Factors

Ignorance of People

This factor actually feeds into many of those that follow. If we don't know who the people around us really are, we'll inadvertently do things that cause negative reactions, and we'll fail to spot the destructive actions when they first begin to appear. The substitute for knowing people—the actual, individual people with whom we have deliberately and perhaps mistakenly surrounded ourselves—is to put them into boxes and imagine them as simplistic pesonality types. Not knowing them will also make it easier to abuse and eliminate them, to count them of little worth—the view of generals who think of their troops as symbols on a board rather than as flesh and blood.

Suggested Solution: Once each quarter, or better, once a month, have a one-on-one time out with each of your people, or at least each of your key people (and certainly all of your direct reports). Do it away from the workplace, over a meal and without time pressure. Start talking to set the stage, then stop talking except to ask questions. Meet with those further down the line at least twice a year in the smallest groups possible, the best group size for this being two—you and the other person. The main goal isn't to get ideas or find out about problems; the goal is knowledge of a complex human being.

And be especially concerned about subordinates who can terminate people without emotion. Real knowledge of people should make firing hard to do in most cases.

The Status Quo

Organizations in which not much is happening or changing are excellent incubators of destructive power. People have a lot of time on their hands and, worse, not enough intellectual stimulation to keep their minds occupied with real needs and challenges. This is one of the deadliest flaws of bureaucracies, and leads to gossip mills, fretting over turf, and petty warfare.

Suggested Solution: No matter how stable your competitive environment (including the absence of competition in government or not-for-profit organizations), never let a sense of the status quo settle in. Watch for the telltale signs: comments like "This is the way we do things" or its uglier sibling, "This is the way we've always done it"; low levels of energy in the atmosphere (you really can tell); or the feeling that everything is routine.

Find ways to shake things up—not just to improve operations, but to destroy this breeding ground of destruction. Create strategic disequilibrium. Reward constant innovation; have employees track all their innovative ideas, whether big or small, in a log that will be used as part of their performance evaluation.

Recognition for Low Risk

We should always be thankful when our people do anything, even just their "job." But we need to be very careful not to reward and recognize people for doing the ordinary, the routine, the activities that are without any risk to themselves. It encourages people who are nonperforming destroyers to fake performance in order to be recognized, and to gain prestige. Prestige, in James Hillman's words, is "illusion like a juggler's trick, leading to the meanings of deception and imposture . . . to uncover where prestige is ruling, look for juggling, deception, pomp and trappings, a desperate fervor to seize and hold office, and not much real risk."[1]

Suggested Solution: Make sure that recognition is given out generously but prudently, like a treasure. Don't use it too often or you'll cheapen the value of the currency. Review your reward/recognition programs to ensure that they elevate only truly value-adding performance, especially a risky one, and not just the "brilliant" comment or report.

Crucifixion Culture

Many organizations are consumed with the twin games of delegating blame and deflecting responsibility. A significant number of companies should replace the "Inc." after their names with "CYA." It usually starts at the top, with visionless, spineless leaders who can't admit their own errors or the contributions they make (through omission or commission) to the errors of others. The worst, ironically, are often those control freaks who want to micromanage others. They deflect responsibility from themselves through verbal gymnastics, playing dumb and, most often, delegating blame. This becomes an organizational pattern: Something went wrong; it's not my fault; it's somebody's fault; it must be yours. This may not be the most damaging form of destructive power, but it's probably the most common. It's at its deadliest when it works against taking risks; usually, the higher the risk, the less likely that anyone in this culture will take it.

Suggested Solution: Make it an organizational policy that no employee may ever delegate blame to anyone else ever again. This should be joined by the corollary policy that all employees are expected to be adults, to take responsibility for what they do wrong as well as for what they do right, and to take ownership of problems rather than burying them (we have, by the way, just covered about half of the required policy manual). Let people know that the only game they'll be punished for in your organization is playing the doubleheader of deflecting responsibility and delegating blame.

Public Criticism

"Praise publicly, criticize privately" is one of the best-known but least used of leadership maxims.

Criticizing people publicly is in itself a destructive use of power. Its goal is to inflict pain and humiliation, along with elevating the "perfect" criticizer (the really subtle experts in this do some minor insincere criticizing of themselves to set the stage). Make no mistake about it: Public criticism *kills* people.

It does get people's attention. And their anger. And their hatred. And their desire for revenge. And, in some cases, their following in the criticizer's footsteps with other people in the organization—and, if they have them, with their kids.

Suggested Solution: We have to be careful, because we do want an environment where people can disagree, challenge ideas, and stop us in a march of folly. But we have to ban—completely, totally, forever—the "right" to criticize other individual human beings in public. No exceptions. And it isn't hard to understand the difference between public disagreement with ideas and public criticism of people.

For five years, I volunteered in a not-for-profit organization to lead, on a part-time basis, a large group of teenagers. I had only two rules: First, no baloney on my watch; and second, no public criticism of me or each other; in other words, they had to treat each other with dignity and respect. In five years, with thirty to forty kids, one "couple" tried to break rule one (they didn't get that far), but nobody broke rule two. They got it. Your people can too, even though they're adults.

Group Punishment for Individual Offenses

Few things are as maddening as being punished as part of a group for something you didn't have any part in. Group punishment for individual offenses is, just like public criticism, a destructive use of power in its own right.

It can take many forms: One person misuses a cash advance, so we eliminate advances or make getting them a torturous project; one person makes a mistake, which generates a whole new policy or procedure for everyone (there really are people who think you can legislate against mistakes); one person abuses the informal "comp time" policy, and comp time is eliminated. It's the easy way, the lazy way, and the wrong way. People seldom forgive organizations when they're unfairly punished, and it turns their hearts toward getting some of the loss back or at least exacting some kind of toll. This big use of destructive power breeds a host of small destructive offspring.

Suggested Solution: Fight to keep policies and procedures to a minimum (we should consider replacing the term *policy and procedure manual* with *policy and procedure 3 × 5*). Never let a few isolated events trigger a new policy or procedure. Have the courage and take the time to deal with the violators individually, and insist that your people do the same. Resist the temptation to use the "extreme" words: "This department *never* finishes its projects"; "this group *always* manages to lose its more-demanding customers." Consider whether punishment is even the right or most effective solution to the problem—or even if the action really was a problem; maybe the violated policy needed to be violated.

Broken Promises

Does it seem to you, as it does to me, that people can't at times remember their commitments for twenty-four hours, but they can remember your promises to them for decades?

But that's the reality. People will remember our promises. Breaking promises is an invitation to discouragement and a birthing room of destructive power—sarcasm, cynicism, undercutting, and taking it out on the organization (in ways like reducing effort or leaving problems unaddressed). It also teaches by example, and the organization's "commitment rate," which should be about 100 percent, will plummet toward zero.

Suggested Solution: Make few promises and make them smaller than what you think you'll really be able to deliver. Underpromise and overdeliver. Create an environment in which people feel free to make promises to each other, because they know they'll be *able* to keep them and be expected to do so, too.

Few feelings in my corporate life were worse than when I had made a commitment to someone else that was well within my territory of operation to make, and then had that commitment overturned, often for the flimsiest, pettiest, or most political of reasons. It's hard not to hate the person who does the overturning. If it happens more than a few times, it's hard not to hate the whole organization.

Cognitive Dissonance

When we require people to perform activities that they find morally repugnant or that otherwise offend their sensibilities, we've opened the door to destructive power. The power can take several forms. They might so resent what we've forced them to do that they'll turn their guns against the organization while they're still there and drop the really big bombs after they've gone. Or they might simply abandon their value system and start operating "pragmatically" (read: "ruthlessly"). A fearsome fury is unleashed when we tell people that what they believe doesn't matter.

Suggested Solution: Learn what the moral and value base of your people is. At the very least, learn what kinds of things offend them and stay clear of asking them to do these things. Stay far away from actions that will offend almost everyone, such as firing someone they don't believe should be fired, doctoring records, or not reporting an overcharge to a customer. Ask: Do I really want people working for me who have been stripped of their principles? "Perhaps the greatest moral benefit that the powerful can bestow on their adherents," writes Robert Dilenschneider, "is to give them the right to do work that is not in conflict with their personal moral agenda."[2]

Absence of Appeal

No system is perfect. All leaders are imperfect. Nobody, really, knows very much, compared with the total of what can be known. An organization lacking the means to appeal poor, misinformed, wrong, or immoral decisions and directives has created a forum for the abuse of power. People in authority will know that there is no way for others to get around them—always a bad situation in human communities. And with no acceptable way to plead their case or resolve their grievances, people will become bitter and discouraged. Bitter and discouraged people have a much harder time acting in the interest of the organization.

Suggested Solution: Fear the destructive potential of leaders who can't be challenged. Build safeguards into the organization. Create a formal grievance system that protects the rights of the griever, the people in authority, and the organization. Let people know that this channel will not be used as a means to bash other people and slow down progress. Balance the need for a respected chain of command with the need for a respected truth. Remember that there's no telling how many good ideas have died and how many bad ideas have been perpetuated because there was no safe way to say "excuse me, but. . . ."

Constant Reorganization

For too many organizations, the answer to problems has been to reorganize.

It's probably such a popular "solution" because it's so visual; it really looks like something is happening. Everything seems new, change is everywhere. But aside from the fact that it is more often than not illusion—reorganization isn't the solution because structure isn't the problem—it's deadly on other grounds. It creates an organizational culture in continual, unnecessary flux that invites manipulation. And people are afraid, so they spend their power on securing their positions and building personal alliances.

Suggested Solution: If patriotism is the last refuge of a scoundrel, then perhaps reorganization is the last refuge of a leader with no real answers. Realize that reorganization is often a smokescreen, and seldom the first or best answer. Use it sparingly. Allow a lot of time between major reorganizations (for instance, "four score and . . ."). Better yet, create a fluid, flexible organization with leaders who follow and followers who lead as needed, so there's no organization definable enough to *be* reorganized.

Unsupportable Promotion Policy

Few organizational actions proclaim more loudly the organization's values than the way it makes—and doesn't make—promotions.

Promoting someone whom nobody believes is worthy of the promotion is akin to driving a dagger into the heart of the organization. "What were they thinking?" "How could they let somebody like that have more authority?" "I thought I knew what this place was made of." It tells the good and the true to give it up, they'll never make it. Some people will start doing what the unworthy person did; after all, it worked for him, didn't it? Others will simply start doing their own thing, or work to make the new leader fail.

Not promoting the person deemed worthy, often because the wrong person has already taken the position, is a more subtle error but has an equal potential for disaster. The bypassed person, if a person of quality, may not turn to destructive power. Those not so principled may. Others noting the oversight will lose respect for the organization. Some of those will turn their disrespect into destructive action.

Suggested Solution: Realize that leaders can't be created by fiat. Leaders can effectively lead only those who acknowledge their right to lead. We can't put promotions up to a vote (or can we?), but we can take the time to know who, if anyone, our people respect, and who they don't. If leadership is, in part, understanding the aspirations of followers and incorporating them into the organization's vision, then perhaps a person worthy of becoming a formal leader should be someone people aspire to follow, someone who embodies their dreams, as well as those of the organization.

Favoritism

We all have "favorites." It's impossible to be human and not have favorites. We like some people more than we like others. Some we like a whole lot more. It's when we translate that liking into granting them something—authority, money, benefits—that we get into trouble. We do this because the "liking" can create a "halo effect," whereby the favorites' performances are seen in a better light than they really are—or their defects are overlooked.

Favoritism can induce the favorites to act in harmful ways because there is a "protection" margin. The favorites can start speaking beyond their scope or authority, and people will respond because they see the connection to us and assume that we agree with these favorites. And some of those not so favored will work very hard to make the favorites look bad, thwart them, and generally wreck their days and careers. Teacher's pets learned this brutal truth long ago. Finally, favoritism will lead us into making some really destructive decisions related to our favorites for the simple reason that no one in his right mind will tell us about the favorites' defects.

Suggested Solution: Take steps to get objective evaluations of the people you really like. If the connection is totally obvious, you'll probably have to do this anonymously.

High Turnover

High rates of employee turnover have a lot of negative implications. One of those is surely the opportunity it creates for destructive power to take root and spread.

A destroyer with even a little seniority can really take advantage of new employees. He can take them under his wing, misdirect them, sour them, poison them against the organization. The high turnover rate itself becomes proof of the organization's perfidy.

Suggested Solution: Learn what's causing the high turnover and take steps to reduce it. Assign new people to a positive mentor/coach for forty-five to ninety days after hiring. Determine to "turnover" the destroyers and retain the builders.

Reduction in Benefits

The Lord may give, and the Lord may take away.

But we'd better not.

Yes, entitlement thinking is noncompetitive, air-headed, and unjust. But, at the same time, taking away something that we've been giving to people feels to them like . . . well, stealing. A reduction in benefits is fertile ground for negativism and the wielding of destructive power.

Suggested Solution: Give benefits slowly. Take them away even more slowly. If you have to reduce them, involve everyone in the process. Help people see why they must be reduced. Let them help determine what form the reductions should take. There's no limit to the amount of good leaders can do if they keep their hands out of people's bank accounts.

Disconnection Between Means and Ends

It's astonishing how often we can want one thing and yet set up a system to get quite something else.

For example, a profit-making organization generally wants, as at least one of its major goals, to make a profit. And then we set up systems that take our eyes off profits. We talk about "revenues" and "revenue growth." We pay commissions based on sales rather than profitability (we ought to call it "making a profit" rather than "making a sale"). And we spend resources on countless things that add no value and hence bring no profit.

Suggested Solution: Alignment. Align ends and means. Review the alignment regularly. "What do we want? Will this system get us that?" It's too easy to reorganize and reengineer without asking the critical question, "Will this add value?" Alignment is an important organizational principle. The alignment of ends and means may be the most crucial of all.

External Factors

There are several external factors that can pave the way for destructive power.

Outsiders Inside

Although it is sometimes necessary to do so for a variety of reason (including getting a fresh perspective), bringing in leadership from the outside also ignites fear, resentment, and, in many cases, opposition.

Suggested Solution: Have outsiders meet with many of your current employees *before* you hire them. Get a reading from your people. Immerse them so much in the decision-making process that the outsider no longer feels like an outsider to them.

Cutthroat Competition

When outside competition gets really fierce, it can press us to act in ways that are not really "us."

Suggested Solution: Focus on your own organization's strengths and values. Set your own standards of excellence and plans of action and then follow them. Innovate to revise the basis of the competition.

●

We've reviewed some of the key factors that can produce destructive power, and the kinds of environment in which destructive power can flourish.

One additional factor brings us back to the second section of this book: an excess of power. Too much power—power beyond what is needed to attain a goal or beyond what people are equipped to handle—is a breeding ground for destructive power. When power reaches a level at which it feels "sovereign," personal ambition and a conviction of superiority can take over, blinding the power holders to their own limitations and the reality that surrounds them.

This is a great danger, for example, to business owners, and an even greater danger to the family members who inherit the power without having to understand where it came from or how hard it is to use constructively. The generation of leadership that follows a destructive founder will, without a major change, be even more destructive than the founder was. It's the law of generational momentum. Bad leadership becomes an offshoot of bad parenting.

But the good news is that destructive power doesn't have to win. It is a powerful entity and shouldn't be underestimated, although it will work hard to get us to do that very thing. But its victory is never assured. Our destiny is what we make it.

And our fate is what we choose.

Notes

1. James Hillman, *Kinds of Power: A Guide to Its Intelligent Use* (New York: Currency Doubleday, 1995), p. 122.
2. Robert L. Dilenschneider, *On Power* (New York: HarperBusiness, 1994), p. 198.

Section IV
Living the Balance

18

Powersharing

I have come to realize the importance of community.
Where I once praised *independence,* I now stress *inter-dependence.*

— M. Scott Peck, psychiatrist
and author

Andrea, after much thought and study, decided to share more power with her nine employees.

"I understand that I've been limiting our effectiveness by holding on to too much power," she told them at an early morning breakfast meeting. "By requiring all customer requests for contract changes to go back through me, I realize that I've been absorbing too much of your time, taking too long to get the customer satisfied, and limiting both your creativity and our ability to meet our customers' needs. From now on, things are going to be different." She went on to outline the new latitude she was granting them.

She felt good about her new direction. She received a lot of positive feedback from her employees and from several of her customers. She was concerned that two of the nine still kept bringing all of their change requests to her. She tried to encourage them, but they seemed paralyzed by and afraid of having more power. Furthermore, she still found herself fighting fires on a daily basis. She decided to be patient.

Other problems took longer to surface, but when they did they left Andrea discouraged and angry.

Jerod, one of her most intelligent subordinates, had ap-

proved some large changes that left Andrea facing substantial losses. He had, in fact, approved every change request made by his customers without getting any additional money. "You told me I had the authority to do it," he said with some surprise when Andrea confronted him on it.

With Robert it was much worse.

Andrea became aware that Robert, her most brilliant employee, was feeding customers internal information and suggesting change requests to at least one of the largest. When she called him into her office, he cut the meeting short by announcing that he had accepted a position with that large customer and was giving notice. Andrea was stunned and enraged.

What happened to Andrea's noble idea of sharing power?

She hadn't learned how to balance it.

The Balance of Power

We've been looking closely at power as a tool and the need to have it balanced in a powersharing arrangement. We've described what a shortage will do (create dependence and the death of initiative) and what an excess will do (create independence and the death of collaboration). We've discussed the importance both of retaining power and of sharing it. And we've analyzed how to draw power out of the right hands and keep it out of (or get it out of) the wrong hands.

Then comes the balancing part.

The first goal is to make an intelligent distribution of power or, to say it another way, to create an exceptional environment where people are free to exchange the power that lies dormant within them at the right times and in the right ways.

The second goal is to avoid the pitfall—and it's a big one—of trying to control the power once we've unleashed it. If we look at it as a transfer of a priceless commodity that these lunkheads are almost certain to make disastrous use of, then we're really not going to let go. We're going to cling to the power even as we talk the language of powersharing. This hypocrisy will push people toward either dependence or independence, depending on the particulars of the situation and the personalities of the people.

This leads to the third goal: to focus and direct the power in conformity with a mutually agreed-upon vision so that all (or at least most) of the power in the organization moves in the same direction. Adam Smith used the metaphor of the "invisible hand," and that is what a communal vision is. Our goal is to have all our free and powerful people moving in the same direction, guided by an invisible seduction. We have to seduce the power by a compelling dream.

Should this vision, this compelling dream, start at and come from the top, or should it grow as a consensus of organizational opinion? *Yes.* It can't be a "chicken or egg" kind of thing, where we create it one way or the other. It has to be both—chicken *and* egg, around and around, honing and shaping, forging a vision that is unique, beneficial, and profitable.

And we as leaders need to be a living, breathing, walking example of that vision. As James Hillman writes, "What ultimately gives one the power of leadership is a capacity to *embody* visionary ideas."[1]

The Redemption of Power

Power has a bad reputation because too many people abuse it and too few understand it. But without it, nothing gets done. We need to embrace constructive power as surely as we abhor destructive power. We need to learn how to use it and to teach our people what we learn. And we need to share it, as the preferred course, in spite of mistakes, in spite of abuses, in spite of misunderstandings. Power shared well is power multiplied, and strong leaders will do it instinctively and willingly.

What do we mean by "redemption of power"? To redeem something means to buy it back. One of the ways we can buy things back is with our efforts and sacrifices. Whenever we use something well after it has frequently been used badly against us and around us, we buy it back. We bring it back to value. We redeem it. Power has often been used for harm, but we can redeem it.

Power is redeemed on the basis of three criteria:

1. *First, and most important, is the purpose for which the power is used.* Is it used to move us a step closer to our organizational vision and goals? Will this use benefit us in the short run, but kill us in three years? Will people be more or less able to work effectively after this power is exercised?

2. *Next in importance is how the power is acquired.* Do I have a clear allocation of power? If I don't, am I willing to take the legitimate steps to get it? Am I unwilling to trample on others, play political games, or compromise my convictions to secure more?

3. *Finally, power is redeemed by how it is shared.* Since it's difficult for a group to exercise more power than the leader has available, groups hoping to be effective should want their leaders to have as much power (latitude, excellent people, and other resources) as might be necessary to accomplish their mission. And one of the most compelling reasons to acquire power is to pass it along, to powershare with those around us at the maximum level.

The ideal person to work for is someone who secures power through legitimate means, uses it to make decisions when necessary, shares it whenever possible, and always has in mind the goal of enhancing the organization. And achieving its vision.

We can be that person.

Wrestling With the Balance

At the beginning of this chapter, we presented the disastrous attempt at powersharing by a well-intentioned leader named Andrea. Where did she go wrong?

First, she made the common and fatal mistake of powersharing with everyone equally. Some people were not prepared to accept their newly acquired freedom and authority, and simply handed the power granted them back to Andrea at every opportunity in the form of waiting, asking questions, and letting problems turn into fires. Given authority and freedom, they chose to disempower themselves. Andrea missed the reality that power is a commodity, like responsibility, raises, and promotions, and must be distributed with care and discretion—and in unequal measure. She needed to give power to those "whose lives are functional products of personal decisions rather than of external decisions."[2]

Second, she didn't give clear enough guidelines about the *limits* of the power she was sharing. She didn't define what she meant, and she didn't define what she *didn't* mean. She assumed that people would do the right thing, and she trusted them too much.

Third, Andrea didn't see that some people, like Jerod, would use the power to make themselves look good and to make their lives easier. He wasn't stealing from the company directly, but in a very real sense he was using his power to serve himself at the organization's expense. There are a lot of people who will do this. They need to be *disempowered,* not allowed to exercise even more power.

And fourth, she didn't see that some people, like Robert, will use their power unethically to advance themselves—over the corpse of the organization if necessary. Someone at a seminar I was giving described one of his employees as "the pure essence of evil." These people need more than disempowerment; they need *disengagement.* They can't be limited. They will draw power to themselves, absorb it, twist it, and use it like a blunt instrument to smash our vision to pieces.

To be effective, we need to powershare. But when doing something that has such potential for misuse, we've got to do it with something akin to mathematical precision.

The leader who wrestles with the balance needs to ask a number of critical questions about power:

- How much do I really have?
- What are its sources and drivers?
- How much do the people around me already have?
- What are its sources and drivers?
- How much do they need?
- How much should I retain and how much should I yield?
- How do I draw it out of the right people and keep it going?

- How do I take it away and keep it away from the abusers?
- How do I balance the power throughout my organization?
- How do I keep the balance over time?

Ongoing Redemption

These aren't questions that can be asked and answered once and for all. The mix is dynamic, involving new people, new ideas, new relationships, rising and falling stars. The effective leader will constantly analyze the level and quality of powersharing, and continually reevaluate the balance of power—where it is, where it should be increased, where it should be decreased.

We need to build striving for a balance of power into the culture of the organization. We need to build a culture in which the movement toward a balance of power and interdependence becomes to some degree inevitable. As John Case concludes, "Through the symbols and practices that give it life, the right culture solves a company's most critical competitive problems . . . powerful cultures have powerful effects on how a company's people work together."[3]

The symbols and practices have to deliver simple, meaningful messages. One of the most important messages that we as leaders can and should reinforce is that nobody has all the power, because nobody has all the answers. And everybody brings something to the table. We share power here. We multiply it. As General Mills has said in its statement of corporate values, "Employees choose General Mills because we reward innovation . . . and release their power to lead." And we work interdependently; we use our power to produce a collaborative enterprise driven by powerful individuals. Nobody can be dependent, and nobody can be independent. We're responsible. We use part of the power we have to take initiative and carry our own loads; we use the rest of our power to help others carry the burdens that are too heavy for one person alone to handle.

We have to reward powersharing and interdependent thinking and actions. We should be shocked and offended when people monopolize and misuse power, block progress and inhibit constructive power, and don't work to inform or help others.

When we've worked at it consistently for a while, we will have built something that many have longed to have but few have been able to create. Hard-won interdependence will redeem and expand our collective power.

We need to think about what today's balance of power, or lack of balance, will do to our organization over the next five years. This includes asking and answering some crucial questions about the future:

- Are we willing to live with the current level of interest and involvement that our people are displaying?
- Can we survive only on what we at the top know or can learn?
- Will the best people stay if we don't powershare with them fully?
- What will our people do if they have too little power? Too much power?
- Can we survive if a substantial amount of our available organizational power is used destructively?
- How should we detect and go about disempowering wielders of destructive power?
- How can we keep power from flowing to those who want it for their personal advancement rather than to those who want to use it for the general good?

Only by asking, and reasking, these questions and answering them very specifically can we hope to maintain a roughly accurate balance of power.

When a person or group has been released to use power, possibilities for current improvement and future leverage are increased dramatically. A new life force has been introduced into the organization.

If nurtured, our success will reverberate through the corridors of shared power.

Notes

1. James Hillman, *Kinds of Power: A Guide to Its Intelligent Use* (New York: Currency Doubleday, 1995), p. 155.

2. Stephen R. Covey, *Principle-Centered Leadership* (New York: Simon & Schuster, 1991), p. 23.

3. John Case, "Corporate Culture," *Inc.*, November 1996, pp. 44, 47.

19

Six Trends That Affect the Balance of Power in the Workplace

The world is ruled by power.
—Tadeusz Borowski, Polish
short story writer

Very little in our culture remains the same for very long, including how the balance of power will "look" as major trends weave their way into the workplace.

The principles of the balance of power, however, will remain the same, because people will remain the same. The way powersharing is handled will always in part determine how much an organization achieves, or whether it achieves anything at all.

Change and Evolution

Change has always been a part of life. The speed of change varies, and the change can be bad or good, but change is the constant. The changes always seem to be new, but a surprisingly high percentage of them are old ideas recycled in new packages.

Our responses to change—at least our first, reflexive responses—are often amazingly like the ways others before us have responded to new things in their lifetimes.

Once we understand that much change is in the direction of where things have been before, and that much response to change is highly predictable, we can structure our organization's culture in such a way that the negative impacts are minimized and the positive impacts are leveraged into opportunity.

Whether or not we believe in biological evolution, we can't wait for it to save us. The often uplifting and pleasurable-to-watch future of *Star Trek,* in which poverty, crime, and war have been eliminated, is an unlikely scenario no matter how many hundreds of years are allowed for it to come to pass. (I'm not too comforted anyway, what with Borg and Klingons and Cardassians and Ferangi, all of which look like the worst of human nature in a different life form.)

Even the evolution of a single life, from immaturity to responsibility and from folly to sound decision making, is incredibly slow, painstakingly slow. We can't wait for people to change, to become excellent on their own initiative, to bring us success.

We've got to understand the changes that are coming, anticipate the likely response, and not hope for people to become more advanced to make the change more palatable. The changes are here today, and we've got to get our organizations ready to incorporate them so that we can use these changes to enhance, rather than destroy, the balance of power.

Six Major Trends

There are at least six trends that will have a significant effect on the balance of power in the coming years. These are not fads, which come and go. These are true trends, which will work their way through the marketplace for many years to come.

Continued and Varied Immigration

People in many of the top global economies today are very worried about immigration.

This is nothing new. People have *always* been worried about immigration. "What will these people do to our nation's culture?" "Will they take our jobs?" "Will they load up the welfare rolls?"

When people sweat about immigration, they're worried about the people who are coming in *now.* Yet most of us reading these words are either descended from immigrants or are immigrants ourselves. Based on that fact alone, most of us should be in favor of immigration. Sometimes, as in the case of Mexican immigrants to the United States, the immigrants are moving to where their ancestors once lived. If we go back far enough, we find that it's their land and that the *rest of us* are the immigrants.

I grew up in a bigoted environment. Bigoted about race, bigoted about ethnic origin, bigoted about economic class (above and below). I consider such attitudes reprehensible. I'm still bigoted, though—bigoted about destroyers, bigoted about bigots. They are horrible people who will demolish the balance of power. We need to distance ourselves from them and keep them out of our organizations. And they come in all colors, shapes, and sizes, and with varying pedigrees.

What the bigots don't understand is that we actually need *more* immigration. "We're letting in only around 900,000 people a year," argues David Birch. "We could easily admit 2 or 3 million people a year—skilled people only, people with a university degree. And if we did that, we could double the growth of the American economy."[1]

Immigration is here to stay. In a global economy that has become much less restrictive, the pace of immigration will probably quicken and the directions will adjust over time. We can dread it and fight against it, or we can strategize to take advantage of it.

It isn't, of course, just a question of bigotry. Other factors come into play. But the large part that *is* bigotry needs to be assaulted.

How will immigration affect the balance of power? We will have to become aware of how other cultures view power, and how these cultural perceptions affect people's comfort with power, their willingness to yield to it, and their willingness and ability to share it. People from some cultures may be more willing than others to powershare and even lean toward independence, while those from repressive or communal cultures may lean toward being told what to do and dependence. Strong cultures permeate our worldviews and may lead some, for example, to wield destructive power without realizing that it's harmful or that it's wrong to do so.

Suggestions:

• Build an organizational culture that values the backgrounds and contributions of all current and future members of the organization. This doesn't mean that all values are equally good (we can pick out the best parts but leave out culturally accepted lying, cheating, oppression, and so forth). It does mean that we lose the false pride and prejudice that advance nothing but do bring much limitation and harm.

• Try to leverage the diversity into a competitive advantage. The balance of power works best when many strong and varied views are brought to the table. It may be harder to balance the power when great diversity is involved, but if we can pull it off, the resulting mix can make our organization uniquely effective.

• Capitalize on the backgrounds of people who come from interdependent cultures, and mix in a healthy blend of people from dependent and independent cultures. Selecting people and matching them to the right assignments and teams will become more difficult, but the success of the resultant product can far exceed that of a largely homogeneous mass.

• Provide the necessary training in your language and culture to enable recent immigrants to work to their full potential. And while you're at it, require the rest of your staff to study the culture of the immigrants. Why should understanding and learning move in only one direction?

I, for one, am glad that people are trying so hard to get into Western countries. Many people think we should set up barriers to keep them out of our individual nations. But what a wonderful problem for a nation to have! Why? In many countries, people are trying hard to get *out,* and their governments have set up barriers to keep them *in.* I'd rather live in a place for which people are willing to take risks to get in than in a country where people have to take risks to get out. We'll know our nation is in serious trouble if the day ever comes when people want to leave more than they want to stay.

The Dominating Influence of Baby Boomers

It's a present reality and an inevitable, actuarial fact over the next twenty years: Baby boomers, like it or not, are in control.

This is good. And this is not so good.

It's good because early in our development we boomers got the idea that we were "all in this together." Even those of us who didn't live in communes were somehow implanted with the idea that the world was interconnected and that no one is an island. This conviction can work well in advancing a collaborative culture and a spirit of interdependence.

It's bad for a number of reasons. Much of this generation was co-opted by the materialistic boom of the 1980s and 1990s. People who once despised the "plastic" culture (as defined forever in *The Graduate,* when an old materialist told Dustin Hoffman the meaning of life in hushed tones: "plastics") are now gleefully using plastic to buy whatever they want. We were set up for this hedonism in part by the previous generation, which in an understandable reaction against the Great Depression determined that "our children will have more than we did." We want power, but we're less excited about its related responsibilities.

It's bad, too, because we're the generation that inherited the maximum fragmentation of society. Western societies have been on the move for many years, but since World War II have become almost nomadic in lifestyle and orientation. Tradition gave way, community gave way, stability gave way. All that was left was the "nuclear family," and now it, too, has given way. The efforts at building "teamwork" and "cooperation" in the schools are too little and too late to cancel out all the social forces working against community and interdependence, at least for this generation.

The defining time for many baby boomers was the 1960s, which historian Paul Johnson has called the most radical decade since the 1790s. We can look at films of protests and concerts and love-ins, and it can look like an era that came and went. But it didn't go. Its effects, both good and bad, are deep and driving. Some of them are:

- An openness to appeals for community and interdependence
- A willingness to call injustice by its name and work against it
- A desire to make a significant difference
- A longing to be treated as "whole" people and to live a multidimensional, soulful life

- A distrust of those in formal positions of authority
- A distrust of authority, period
- A strong narcissism ("If it feels good, do it") that can slip into hedonism
- An oversimplification of both problems and solutions

The wise leader will be aware of these underlying attitudes and will take account of their subtle power when dealing with this generation—and really, in some ways, with those that follow.

Suggestions:

- Use the modern realities of complexity and disconnectedness, which are hitting the baby boomer generation hard. As time goes on, they will be hitting the boomers even harder, and a backlash already taking root will flourish. We can appeal to this backlash with a message of a simpler life, shared power, interdependence, and losing the relentless drive to get . . . somewhere.
- Appeal to the sense of social justice that at one time permeated this generation. Sharing power, utilizing people's best skills, and building a culture in which my weaknesses are offset by another's strengths can be cast in the light of community and social justice, where we all have respected voices, and none of us are disqualified by anyone but ourselves.
- Offer the interdependent organization as a partial substitute for the connectedness that is missing from so many lives. We can never pretend that the workplace is a family, because it isn't. But the interdependent organization can offer some sense of constancy, of "home base," in an atomized culture.

The Needs and Desires of Generation X

Is this really the generation that believes in nothing? Or is it just an honest generation having to find the answers on its own?

In all honesty, much of what was claimed to be a "moral world" never really was. It was just presented that way by the pretensions of hypocrisy. But now all that is gone. A recent survey showed that 71 percent of generation Xers believe "In this world, sometimes you have to compromise your principles."[2] The truly sad part is that much of this generation has grown up not being taught and shown the critical values of successful and honorable living, and in many cases has been taught that there aren't any. The good part is that the hypocrisy has been vaporized (or at least seen for what it really is), and there is a lot of energy in generation X to find and to live by some real values. This generation deeply wants genuineness and authenticity. These would be wonderful virtues to have more of in our organizations, which can be so encumbered with illusion and denial. Perhaps their search can help drive our own quest as leaders to build our organizations on reality and truth.

This generation is really disconnected, but it doesn't want to be. Perhaps the very level of disconnectedness produces the longing for something connected, something collaborative, something mutual. Although the boomers are feeling the backlash against complexity and disconnectedness, much of the backlash is actually being driven by their children.

I hear many complaints from leaders (and parents) about generation X, but I have to say that I think there's a lot there to be helped along and drawn from. I like these people. Their self-reliance, flexibility, and resilience are excellent characteristics to possess in today's marketplace. It would be a waste, both for them and for our organizations, to ask the age-old question in the age-old tone: "What's *wrong* with this younger generation?" Sometimes *wrong* just means "different." Let's focus on what's right first. And then we'll be in position to use what's wrong as the raw material from which to produce something good.

Does this generation have big problems, or does it have the seeds of greatness?

Yes.

Suggestions:

• This generation of people is poised to belong to something. They also are savvy and willing to take on challenges. Give them meaningful work in the context of a meaningful (to them) vision. Rather than relying on traditional management techniques, we need to talk with them, find out what drives them, and construct and frame our vision in a way that appeals to who they are. We need to think flexibility with this generation. In addition, "several experts say younger workers need faster feedback, more rewards, and continual training to keep them challenged."[3] Only when we have done these things can we powershare with them intelligently and effectively.

• Create an environment that feels like "home." Reading rooms, sun rooms, plants, couches, paintings—we can stop thinking "This is an office" and start thinking "This is a community." Many people are opting out of the corporate world and going into home offices. We can give them the option without forcing them to move. They'll be there and available for powersharing.

• Draw on the different *type* of competitiveness that this generation has. "Wary of institutions, addicted to information, resolutely self-reliant yet dependent on immediacy, this generation of young workers couldn't have been better conditioned to compete in an atmosphere of corporate instability, knowledge capital, worker autonomy, and deadlines," claims Tom Peters.[4] This is a very entrepreneurial generation, with many starting "garage" businesses and making them thrive. It's a competitive spirit that seems more related to finding and exploiting a niche than attacking and destroying others. Learn who they are as individuals and give them work in line with their values and interests; this will feed the initiative side of interdependence. And place them in cooperative ventures and reward them for doing this connecting well; this can feed the collaborative side of interdependence.

The Increasing Pace and Discontinuity of Change

Instability is enough to scare us all to death.

Things are moving so fast for most of us that we can feel at times that our lives are careening recklessly down a mountain and that our voice is just a whisper in a large auditorium.

It's in the midst of this whirlwind that a rock to hide behind can be very appealing. The interdependent organization can be one of those rocks.

Suggestions:

• Form "change response" teams when we face major changes, either from the outside or the inside. Try to involve as many people as possible, preferably everyone, on a response team, with each team looking at a different aspect of the change. People working toward a common goal—understanding and preparing for the change—can build interdependence even in desperate times. Maybe especially then.

• Use the very threat of change and its accompanying instability to draw people closer together. Change causes people to feel disconnected, even alienated. We can use this very aspect of change to move people toward interdependence for their own comfort and survival.

• Clearly illustrate that change has a tremendous power to paralyze us and make us dependent, or to uproot us and make us independent. We can show how taking one or the other of these two courses is the "normal" response, and appeal to our people's deeper side by asking them to develop the thoughtful and unusual response—interdependence.

The Quantity of Knowledge and Information

The amount of information available today exceeds that available to all prior generations. It also exceeds anything that most of us can possibly hope to absorb.

Information glut can drive people both to dependence ("I can't do anything until I get all the data") or independence ("I can learn everything I need to know through my computer— I don't need to talk with anybody" or "I'll never be able to get the data I need anyway, so I'll just do something"). From analysis paralysis to computer arrogance, information can be as much an enemy as a friend.

Computers and the information they spawn can actually be a distraction from true knowledge, not to mention wisdom. This problem begins early on, in grade school. "U.S. teachers," Todd Oppenheimer tells us, "ranked computer skills and media technology as more 'essential' than the study of European history, biology, chemistry, and physics; than dealing with social problems . . . than learning practical job skills; and than reading modern American writers such as Steinbeck and Hemingway or classic ones such as Plato and Shakespeare."[5] We can confuse the quantity of information with knowledge, access with wisdom, and a useful tool (the computer) with *more* useful disciplines and fields of learning.

Only an interdependent acquisition and dispersion of information can turn the glut into a valuable organizational asset.

Suggestions:

• Ask people to share information with others only *after* it has been turned into knowledge. We can bring interdependence into the picture by asking everyone to sort, sift, and add value (knowledge content) to the information before they pass it along.

• Develop collection points where people can "post" what they've learned about what has worked or not worked. To be maximally effective, the information should be posted by topic, so that someone looking for answers can get to them fast.

• Ban useless or destructive forms of information sharing, such as mass distributions, "CYA" documentation, or "look at me" memos. These only drain organizational power and reduce both the spirit and the time needed for interdependent activity.

Changing Perspectives on Values and Virtues

Without question, there has been a dramatic shift in thinking about values in the last few decades.

Some of the change has been good. We needed to move away from archaic and counterproductive ideas about race, women's roles, ambition, and the "American dream" (that is, materialism will make you happy). They were values, but there was nothing virtuous about them.

Other changes have not been so good. There has been a substantial loss of belief in the concept that our lives have a deeper meaning. At the same fundamental level, the ennobling belief that humanity is special and deserves to be treated as such has faded under the onslaught of extreme Darwinism, biological determinism, psychological labels (which often equate unselfishness with "lack of boundaries," and love with "co-dependency"), and religious nonsense (from "The earth is our mother" to "Humanity is completely depraved").

Certainly, people have abused the general belief in humanity's and the individual's specialness by using it as a justification for narcissism and worse. The cult of the self, environmental destruction, ruthless and lawless competition, social and economic injustice, barbaric regimes, and senseless wars have all proved that humanity can be unbelievably base and at times barren of virtue. At the same time, these realities don't negate the view that we are special; they only temper it.

Without the view that humanity is special and that individuals have some kind of matchless worth, we're left to combat horrible behavior with platitudes: "Be kind." "Be respectful." "Be courteous." But why? Why do these things? If there are no higher values or virtues, why not take all you can get, and the devil with the environment, nonhuman life, *human* life, and the future of the earth itself?

The very fact that we are concerned about the environment, endangered species, and the weak and helpless among us is some kind of signal that we *are* special. According to the concept of natural selection and the survival of the fittest, we *should* be wiping out all these "inferior" species that are taking up our space. If they're too weak to defend themselves, we could in a world of pure Darwinism let them die off. Ultimately, we can't have it both ways. Either we're special and that's why we fight against natural selection and survival of the fittest, or we're just another point on the "living being" line and that's why we ought to kill them off before they do it to us.

There *are* higher values. There are principles of life that really work. A truly successful interdependent organization believes this to be so and incorporates them into its culture.

Suggestions:

• People today are lost in a valueless world. Establish your organization on higher ground. Offer them something that they deeply need, including meaningful interaction with others in the accomplishment of worthwhile goals. Our organizations can't be substitutes for spiritual life—but they can be a reasonable part of it.

• Establish ground rules for successful interdependence that can give people a mode of relating that is difficult to find in the world at large. Although they might come without a grid for productive interdependence, they also come with a yearning to have it.

• Make sure that a section of the vision statement covers "principles we are willing to go under for rather than compromise." It is amazing how many of these have been part of the culture of a high percentage of successful, ennobling organizations and nations. If this section is really good, and really practical, people will make copies of it for their family and friends. If this section is superb, it can have the power (like *semper fidelis*, "always faithful") to drive people to go through fire and lay their lives on the line.

If they just make copies, we will have arrived.

●

The organizations most likely to live long and prosper in the years to come are those with a balance of power and a continual focus on interdependence (along with an intense focus on a few core products or services). Some of the major trends will work against this at times, and some will work for it. With leadership, all of them can be made to work for it.

Our mission as leaders in a world of great flux is to make all these trends work to make powersharing and interdependence more of a reality—and more of a triumph.

Notes

1. David Birch, in "Help Wanted," by Michael Hopkins, *Inc.*, July 1997, p. 40.
2. Margot Hornblower, "Great Xpectations," *Time,* 9 June, 1997, p. 62.
3. Stephanie Armour, "Xers Mark the Workplace," *USA Today,* 13 October, 1997, p. 5B.
4. Tom Peters, "Culture Shift," *Fast Forward,* March 1997, p. 1.
5. Todd Oppenheimer, "The Computer Delusion," *Atlantic Monthly,* July 1997, p. 46.

20

The Competitive Advantage of a Balance of Power

It's true that money talks. *But power shouts.*
> —Michael A. Boylen,
> *The Power to Get In,* p. 45

It is important for us to understand that the balance of power is not a "soft" business issue or one that has no effect on the bottom line.

It also isn't optional.

Leaders can accomplish some goals by themselves. Followers can do this, too. But only by balancing the efforts of both groups, only by finding the equilibrium point of power, can we bring maximum results to the necessarily lean, flexible, agile, and hard-to-define organization of the twenty-first century.

Powersharing may not be as obvious a competitive advantage as a hot new product or a service breakthrough, but it's just as real. And a lot longer-lasting.

The Competitive Advantage of Interdependent People

"Intellectual capital will go where it is wanted and stay where it is well treated. It cannot be driven; it can only be attracted."[1]

246 Living the Balance

"Wanted" and "well treated" imply that there is an interconnection with others that is mutually beneficial. Only the interdependent organization is capable of holding on to the very best and brightest people.

We need to reward people for "growing" other people. We need to give people a bonus and recognition when someone they've mentored gets promoted *out* of their area and into another leader's.

Leaders have a key role to play in this structuring. "The key to competitive advantage," according to Bennis and Townsend, "will be the capacity of leadership to create a social architecture capable of generating intellectual capital."[2] The "social architecture" has to include a balance of power and true interdependence if we intend to tap into all of the capability that lies dormant in our organizations.

If we do, we will gain a competitive advantage on many fronts:

- Having more people involved means not only more ideas but more possible combinations of ideas and more people with an interest in making those combinations. We ought to be able to find the good ideas lying in the cracks.
- Reduction in the costs of turnover, namely, recruiting, interviewing, hiring, training. "It is easy to see that effective empowerment can spill over into higher retention rates, better productivity, attraction of good job candidates and more effective team interaction," writes Barbara Ettorre.[3]
- Increased "span of control," or the theoretical number of people someone can "manage." Given self-managed knowledge workers, this number should go way up. (And given the myth of control, it ought to disappear from the leadership literature altogether.)

Finally, to be competitive we've got to quit competing.

Competition for and monopolization of power can kill our organizational competitiveness. "Top-down leaders," argues Sally Helgesen, "by withholding power from those in the ranks, deprive them of the ability to use the expertise and information vested in them to respond directly and with speed to customer concerns. . . . 'The typical result is that a few powerful people have more resources than they actually need, while everybody else has to make do with less. It's static, irrational, and inefficient.' "[4]

The Competitive Advantage of Interdependent Teams

Functional departments that accumulate power and use it to limit the options of others are still very much alive, even though they are killing their host organizations. "Monopoly limits intelligence by taking exclusive power in an area, thus inevitably reducing others' choices, freedom, and initiative."[5]

Mutuality, a hallmark of the interdependent organization, creates a free market in ideas that enhances the ability of the organization to respond to change, take advantage of opportunities, and interact to produce solutions in times of crisis or error.

In times of change, perhaps the foundational need is for imaginative, multidimensional thinking. The solution to many competitive problems lies not in cleverly rearranging the existing elements but rather in "seeing" the problem in entirely new ways, visualizing pieces of the solution that don't yet exist, and jettisoning current components that are in the way, no matter how familiar or comfortable they are. It would be a rare individual who could do this, and even rarer if that person could do it a second time. Thomas Jefferson and Thomas Edison were two such giants. But the well-formed interdependent team can match them—no, *exceed* them—not primarily because of the sum of the intelligences collected together, but because of the incredible effects of the *combination* of intelligences, creating, shaping, adding, deleting, enhancing.

The interdependent team also provides the opportunity to transform one-time events or initiatives into ongoing processes that can produce a marked improvement over time. For example, cost reduction can be a one-time "chop" or, in the hands of teams, a systematic cost-minimization process. As a one-time event, cost cutting: is a unilateral decision; can cut muscle as well as fat; can negatively affect available skills, capability, and "memory"; is difficult to "localize" (that is, cut where costs should be cut); and can build fear and cynicism. A systemic cost-minimization process, by contrast: is a goal that involves everyone on the team; improves the organization continually without devastating it; keeps core competencies intact; and develops a lean attitude in the culture. Interdependent teams can *transform* what individuals can only chip away at.

Why Design an Interdependent Organization?

If we powershare with people, they will make mistakes and cost us some money and some grief. Some will waste their power, and at least a few will abuse it. We powershare with people in spite of these realities, not in some illusory hope that the people we hire will somehow not be . . . people.

Our hope has to be in this: That the cumulative effect of the efforts of many people with power will far outweigh the inevitable losses that will come from mistakes and abuses.

Micromanagers concentrate power in themselves rather than risk the losses, and use their power to control, limit, veto, and terrify. Their power is actually reduced to a molecule and turned into a bad joke, a parody of true power. They eliminate the losses that come from powersharing and, along with them, all the gains as well.

Great leaders powershare freely but very shrewdly. They distribute it in such a way as to maximize the gains and minimize unnecessary losses. And they maintain their optimism in people in spite of the reality that some will let them down. They know that workers with power won't always outperform workers who cower, but workers with the right amount of constructive power will always leave them in the dust.

In summary, we can do what we've outlined in this book, not merely because it's nice or the "right" thing to do. It *is* nice, and it *is* the right thing to do.

But it will also beat the pants off everyone who doesn't do it. And in a lot of ways besides just money.

Notes

1. Walter Wriston, as quoted in *Leadership Trapeze*, p. 23.
2. Warren Bennis and Robert Townsend, *Reinventing Leadership* (New York: William Morrow, 1995), p. 3.
3. Barbara Ettorre, "The Empowerment Gap: Hype vs. Reality," *Management Review*, July/August 1997, p. 13.
4. Sally Helgesen, "Leading From the Grass Roots," as quoted in *The Leader of the Future*, ed. Frances Hesselbein, Marshall Goldsmith, and Richard Beckhard (San Francisco: Jossey-Bass, 1996), pp. 22–23.
5. Gifford and Elizabeth Pinchot, *The Intelligent Organization* (San Francisco: Berrett-Koehler Publishers, 1996), p. 42.

Epilogue

Power must be shared for an organization or a relationship to work.

> —Max DePree, *Leadership Is
> an Art,* p. 105

Powersharing is not a "gimme."

It comes with uncertainties, ambiguities, fears, concerns,
and best efforts gone awry. No matter how wise we are, we will
make some mistakes.

Sometimes we'll retain power when it would be better to
yield it. This will shortchange results and introduce dependence.
Other times we'll yield power when it would be better to hold
onto it. This will sidetrack goals and introduce independence.
We'll work to achieve a balance, and sometimes we'll miss it
widely. Even when we approximate it, it will last only a short
time.

We'll try to powershare with constructive people, and when
we do it well we will, at times, be stunned by the results. Even if
we're careful, we'll sometimes powershare with destructive people, and when we do we will, almost always, be stunned by the
results.

I've tried in this book to sketch the principles and guidelines
for powersharing well. Some of these things will be easier for us
to do than they would be for others, and some will be harder.
But they are all critical to successful powersharing.

The old leadership skills—planning, organizing, staffing,
directing, monitoring, and controlling—were really managerial

skills. Although elements of each of these remain in the reper-toire of the leader, their day of ruling is over. The leader today has a new character. New skills are needed.

In a day of hypercompetition, rapid and breathtaking change, and knowledge-based work, the ability to powershare intelligently has to be near the top of the list. Everyone in our organizations needs to be a manager—a self-manager—and lead-ers need to lead and not manage, except to manage themselves.

In pointing the way to a balance of power, this book asks several important questions that I have tried to answer:

- *Who's got it?* Everybody. Everyone brings power to the table. In many organizations, those in positions of formal author-ity reserve all the power to themselves. They create a power monopoly. Only theirs can be exercised, except by special per-mission (empowerment). Much, if not most, of the power avail-able to the organization (that is, already existing *within* the organization) lies dormant, contributes nothing, is wasted. In a few organizations, powersharing is already a reality. Powershar-ing means using the power available to us in the appropriate mixes and blends to effectively and efficiently achieve our goals. It implies ebbs and flows, leaders sometimes following and fol-lowers sometimes leading.

- *Who wants it?* Everybody. Everyone wants to attain their goals, perform work expertly and with confidence, and have an organizational "voice." Everyone wants to have their work lives count. There's no way to do any of these things without power. Some of those who want power will want it for constructive pur-poses, such as achieving the organization's vision, handling im-portant priorities, creating new directions, building a legacy. But others will want it for destructive purposes, like achieving their own vision, handling important personal priorities, critiquing new directions, and knocking buildings down.

- *Who ought to have it in your organization?* Everybody. Everyone in the long term should be part of our powersharing, because we've weeded out the the abusers who are already here and set up force fields to keep out any new ones. We don't want anyone working for us with whom we can't powershare.

When we've answered these questions carefully, and taken the necessary steps to implement effective powersharing, we'll have one of the undisputable competitive weapons for the decades to come: a balance of power.

I'd like to close by quoting Jim Collins: "The next wave of enduring great companies will be built not by technical or product visionaries but by social visionaries—those who see their company and how it operates as their ultimate creation and who invent entirely new ways of organizing human effort and creativity."[1]

May it be so for you.

●

As we end this part of our journey together, I would consider it a privilege and an honor to hear from you. If you have a comment or question, please feel free to contact me.

James R. Lucas, President
Luman Consultants
P.O. Box 2566
Shawnee Mission, KS 66201
913-248-1733
Fax: 913-671-7728
E-Mail: JLucasLC@aol.com

I'll do my best to give you a response.

Note

1. Jim Collins, "The Most Creative Product Ever," *Inc.*, May 1997, p. 84.

Recommended Reading List

These all have something to say. I've put a * by the ones I'd suggest you start with.

Aubuchon, Norbert. *The Anatomy of Persuasion.* New York: AMACOM, 1997.

Bennis, Warren. *Why Leaders Can't Lead: The Unconscious Conspiracy Continues.* San Francisco: Jossey-Bass, 1989.

Bennis, Warren, and Burt Nanus. *Leaders: The Strategies for Taking Charge.* New York: Harper & Row, 1985.

*Bennis, Warren, and Robert Townsend. *Reinventing Leadership: Strategies to Empower the Organization.* New York: William Morrow, 1995.

Briskin, Alan. *The Stirring of Soul in the Workplace.* San Francisco: Jossey-Bass, 1996.

Brislin, Richard W. *The Art of Getting Things Done: A Practical Guide to the Use of Power.* New York: Praeger, 1991.

Brookhiser, Richard. *Founding Father: Rediscovering George Washington.* New York: Free Press, 1996.

Cohen, Allan R., and David L. Bradford. *Influence Without Authority.* New York: Wiley, 1990.

*Collins, James C., and Jerry I. Porras. *Built to Last: Successful Habits of Visionary Companies.* New York: HarperBusiness, 1994.

Crainer, Stuart. *The Ultimate Business Library.* New York: AMACOM, 1997.

*Covey, Stephen R. *Principle-Centered Leadership.* New York: Simon & Schuster, 1991.

*DePree, Max. *Leadership Is an Art.* New York: Bantam Doubleday Dell, 1989.

Fitz-Enz, Jac. *The 8 Practices of Exceptional Companies: How Great Organizations Make the Most of Their Human Assets.* New York: AMACOM, 1997.

Galbraith, John Kenneth. *The Anatomy of Power.* Boston: Houghton Mifflin, 1983.

Gardner, John W. *On Leadership.* New York: Free Press, 1990.

Goss, Tracy. *The Last Word on Power: Re-invention for Leaders and Anyone Who Must Make the Impossible Happen.* New York: Currency Doubleday, 1996.

Guillory, William A., and Linda A. Galindo. *Empowerment: For High-Performing Organizations.* Salt Lake City: Innovations International, Inc. Publishing Division, 1994.

*Hesselbein, Frances, Marshall Goldsmith, and Richard Beckhard, eds. *The Leader of the Future: New Visions, Strategies, and Practices for the Next Era.* San Francisco: Jossey-Bass, 1996.

Hillman, James. *Kinds of Power: A Guide to Its Intelligent Use.* New York: Currency Doubleday, 1995.

Hitchcock, Darcy, and Marsha Willard. *Why Teams Can Fail and What to Do about It: Essential Tools for Anyone Implementing Self-Directed Work Teams.* Chicago: Irwin, 1995.

Kanter, Rosabeth Moss, John Kao, and Fred Wiersema, eds. *Innovation: Breakthrough Thinking at 3M, DuPont, GE, Pfizer, and Rubbermaid.* New York: HarperBusiness, 1997.

Kepner, Charles H., and Hirotsugu Iikubo. *Managing Beyond the Ordinary.* New York: AMACOM, 1996.

Kidder, Tracy. *The Soul of a New Machine.* Boston: Little, Brown, 1981.

Kotter, John P. *A Force for Change: How Leadership Differs from Management.* New York: Free Press, 1990.

Kotter, John P. *Leading Change.* Boston: Harvard Business School Press, 1996.

Lukes, Steven, ed. *Power.* New York: New York University Press, 1986.

McCoy, Thomas J. *Creating an "Open Book" Organization: Where Employees Think and Act Like Business Partners.* New York: AMACOM, 1996.

Pfeffer, Jeffrey. *Managing with Power: Politics and Influence in Organizations.* Boston: Harvard Business School Press, 1992.

Pinchot, Gifford and Elizabeth. *The Intelligent Organization: Engaging the Talent and Initiative of Everyone in the Workplace.* San Francisco: Berrett-Koehler, 1996.

Ries, Al. *Focus: The Future of Your Company Depends on It.* New York: HarperBusiness, 1996.

Ross, Gerald, and Michael Kay. *Toppling the Pyramids: Redefining the Way Companies Are Run.* New York: Times Books, 1994.

Shapiro, Eileen C. *Fad Surfing in the Boardroom: Reclaiming the Courage to Manage in the Age of Instant Answers.* Reading, Mass.: Addison-Wesley, 1995.

Shorris, Earl. *Power Sits at Another Table and Other Observations on the Business of Power.* New York: Simon & Schuster, 1987.

Simon, Hermann. *Hidden Champions: Lessons from 500 of the World's Best Unknown Companies.* Boston: Harvard Business School Press, 1996.

Stone, Florence M. *The Manager's Balancing Act.* New York: AMACOM, 1997.

Tracy, Diane. *The Power Pyramid: How to Get Power by Giving It Away.* New York: William Morrow, 1990.

*Wellins, Richard S., William C. Byham, and George R. Dixon. *Inside Teams: How 20 World-Class Organizations Are Winning Through Teamwork.* San Francisco: Jossey-Bass, 1994.

Wheelis, Allen. *The Path Not Taken: Reflections on Power and Fear.* New York: W. W. Norton, 1990.

Index